Give America a Chance

The Rants and Raves of an American Patriot

A.J. Nelson

GIVE AMERICA A CHANCE; THE RANTS AND RAVES OF AN AMERICAN PATRIOT

Visit our website at www.GiveAmericaAChance.com

Copyright © 2014 by Cross Current Publishing

Visit our website at www.CrossCurrentPublishing.com

All rights reserved. No part of this book may be reproduced or transmitted in any form or by any means without written permission from the author.

Paperback
ISBN-13: 978-0-9904919-0-3
ISBN-10: 0990491900

E-Book
ISBN-13: 978-0-9904919-1-0
ISBN-10: 0990491919

Made in the United States of America

*To Madison, Jonah, and Caleb,
I pray that this book will impact the
United States of America in a way that will
allow you to enjoy the country that
I grew up loving and fighting for.*

Acknowledgments

God, thank you!

To my wife, Jessica, thank you for standing by my side in this adventure. Thank you for seeking out an American-made journal to make my writing possible. Thank you for painting the "American Flag and Eagle" for my birthday—Almost 6 years later, it became the cover to our book. And finally, thank you for putting up with all of my late nights working. Without your support, none of this would have been possible. I love you more than my words could ever express.

Dad and Mom, thank you for raising me with a strong moral compass, equally matched work ethic, and supporting my creative adventures. I love you both.

Lydia, thank you for your support and encouragement while reading and editing my book. You are a hero and a patriot and I love you very much.

And finally, James, thank you for the number of hours you spent reading, editing, re-reading, proofing, and re-reading again. You're a great friend.

To you, the American patriot reading this book,

It is my honor to say "thank you" for taking a stand for our country.

When you have completed reading this book, please pass it on to a fellow patriot and encourage them to give America a chance!

Sincerely,

A.J. Nelson

Patriot

Pronunciation: ˈpā-trē-ət
Usage: noun
First Known Use: 1605
Definition: a person who loves and strongly supports or fights for his or her country
Full Definition: one who loves his or her country and supports its authority and interests

By permission. From *Merriam-Webster's Collegiate® Dictionary, 11th Edition* ©2014 by Merriam-Webster, Inc. (www.Merriam-Webster.com)

October 1, 2013

A number of things happened that will permanently place this day in my memory…

For starters, this is the day that I started typing up my book, "Give America a Chance; The Rants and Raves of An American Patriot." (Yes, I originally had it written down "old-fashioned-like" with pen and paper). There couldn't have possibly been a better (or worse) day in history to begin this process; I'll tell you why.

For those that remember, it was the first time in years that the US government was in a "so-called" shutdown.

It was also the day that the Affordable Health Care Act, or" Obamacare," opened up the health care exchanges for business… more of that later.

As significant as those events are, what will stick in my mind most of all was the fact that this is the day I made the decision to lay my long-time best friend to rest. Audi, my nearly 15-year-old black Labrador retriever was, well… old. They say that there is only one best dog in the world and every boy owns it. Audi was my best dog in the world. She was by my side for nearly 15 years with the exceptions of a few overseas travels. She deserves a book of her own, but this isn't the book for that.

This book is about another decision I made: on July 4th, 2009, I decided to Give America a Chance. I made the decision to spend one year of my time, and as much as possible of my hard earned cash, on American-made products. In the following pages, you will see my successes, failures, and frustrations (stupid wall sconce!). You'll also be privy to many, if not all, of the thoughts that run through my American patriot mind.

Full disclosure up front though, I was not 100% successful. Although I only spent a year documenting my purchases (or at least a portion of them), this is going to be a lifelong quest. And although I am only one person, my hope, my dream, my expectation of you, is that you will join me by seeking, finding, demanding, and telling others to expect American-made products.

Why? Glad you asked. In 2009, when I first started writing, the national debt of our nation was nearly 12 trillion dollars. A year later, it was approaching 14 trillion dollars. Today, right now, it's $16,959,898,400,907. If it's tough to read, that's because it's **sixteen trillion, nine-hundred and fifty-nine billion, eight-hundred and ninety-eight million, four-hundred thousand, nine-hundred and seven dollars**. By 2017, it expected to well exceed 20 trillion dollars. Why are we continuing to dig deeper and deeper in debt?

These numbers aren't meant to bore you, they're meant to bring you awareness. This is the reason I spent a year documenting my trials. Read on. Join me. Together we can take America back. My ultimate goal is to start turning our debt clock backwards. Republican, democrat, libertarian, whatever, it's not about politics, it's about our country. Our country wasn't built by refusing to negotiate (*cough—congress), it was built by uniting with a common goal. If you're an American, then you have something in common with me. Read on; our challenge is to find U.S. products that work, demand more U.S. products that work, and get America working again.

Well, here we go… Below you will find the exploits of a man who is making an attempt at making this country a better place. Throughout this book, you will find the rants and raves of a man who truly believes in this country. My rants may not be your rants. My raves may not be yours either, but they are the words of a fellow American. I will rave on products that are made in the USA. I will complain about products made elsewhere that I was "forced" to buy. I will issue challenges. Some will be easy, some might really stink, but I dare you to give them a try and see if they don't make your personal life, and more importantly, your country, better.

The first thing you might notice is that the book starts with August 1, 2009. I am fully aware that this is almost 4 years ago. I could list a number of "excuses" as to why I let my book sit on a shelf for a few years, but you'll learn very quickly that this book is as pertinent today as it was in 2009. You'll also learn how quickly history repeats itself, and I think you'll see that it provides a good view of our American future if things don't change.

To show how quickly history repeats itself and how relevant these words play in our modern life, I've added an update to the end of each chapter with a brief commentary. This'll give you the opportunity to read my journal as it was originally written with minimal editing.

August 1, 2009

I am an American patriot! A few weeks ago, I proposed the idea of writing a book documenting my attempts at buying American-made products. The idea of buying all-American products sounds simple enough, but have you taken a look at most merchandise available today? From food to cars to tools (3 of my favorite things), I get all sorts of reactions from salespeople when I ask for an American products. That is what this book is about, along with some of my own rants. [1]

When I told this idea to my wife, she immediately went to Hobby Lobby and purchased a journal to record my daily events, which led to a bit of a story in itself. She, of course, mentioned to the sales clerk that she wanted a journal made in the USA. There on the shelf was a STRATHMORE journal made in Wisconsin, USA… the state of my birth. The sales clerk actually said that the purchasing of American-Made products would make a great book! So, here I sit with my American-made beer and my American-made journal trying to figure out how in the world to write a book!? [2]

You see, it's not that I don't appreciate foreign-made items; it's simply that I am a patriot who loves my country! AND, I firmly believe that American-made products are better than those made in some other countries. I haven't always held this belief, but in my older, more mature state, I've taken some time to compare the products I've bought and those I still own. For example, I have a 2002 Chevrolet Silverado with 165,000 miles on it. In the past, I've owned 1 Nissan truck, 3 Toyota's, 1 Honda, and for a short time, a 1977 Chevrolet pickup. My current Chevrolet blows away the competition. Now, I am not so delusional as to believe my truck was completely made of American parts, but the standard of the parts and overall quality is what makes me a believer in "The American Standard." [3]

Give America A Chance

I can hear the complaints already… "My Toyota or my Honda was built in the USA." Great! But where do the profits go home to? Before the current administration, when I bought my truck, the profits stayed right here…HOME! [4]

I also know that I will not be 100% successful in my attempt to buy all-American products, but that's kind of the point! Why not? If you read this book and go to your local market or store and declare that you want, by choice, American beef or American-made tools, maybe we can stop importing 2nd rate quality products, save money, and enjoy our own top-quality merchandise.

Together, let's stand for what we want. Let's choose, not by law, by choice, to make American greater and stronger. Let's quit exporting jobs and materials and keep it right here. Create jobs for the willing! Pride in what we do! And get that famous "Made in USA" label back on the products we want! Join me, will you? [5]

August 1 Update

1. Years later, with my eyes opened, I can see there are millions of things that are made in the USA. Pretty much anything you would need can be found right here in our great country. Keep your eyes open.
2. This certainly wasn't the first American product purchased in the Nelson household and it will not be the last.
3. I sold my Chevrolet a couple years ago now… It had nearly 200,000 miles and was still running strong. When I decided to purchase a new vehicle, I picked up essentially the exact same truck, a GMC Sierra. I looked at Dodge and Ford. There were certainly aspects of those trucks that I really, really liked, but Chevy still won out in my mind.
4. Lately, GM vehicles have been in the news for some "less than honorable" business practices. I hate to say it, but just because a manufacturer is American doesn't mean they're omitted from dishonesty. I'm not sure what the most recent recalls are going to do for the 2014 statistics, but in recent years, Toyota and Honda have higher recall stats than GM or Ford.

    I've spoken about this with others and the pro's for Toyota or other vehicles built in the USA definitely need strong consideration. With each of those products, even though a large percentage of the profits are sent to another country, there's quite a bit of American workers that have jobs because of them. I can't argue with a company that provides Americans quality jobs.
5. I've heard it over and over from dozens of people that we should demand American-made products… My goal is to encourage millions and millions of Americans to demand American-made products. Demand it!

    I want to dwell on this for just a second… I want the freedoms that America was founded on. The America where Americans are free to choose what they want, choose how they get it (as long as it's ethical), and choose where they get whatever they want. I believe in the power of the people. I believe in the strength of Americans. Read on… You'll see what I mean.

Give America A Chance

August 2, 2009

So it's the second day of writing the book and all I thought about was things I could write down. I could write about church this morning, hummingbird feeders (I'll get to that), friends, family, or wall sconces. What I've decided is just to give you some background on me... after a quick hummingbird story.

I like to watch the hummingbirds drink from the feeder I put up. But sometimes, I get dozens at a time and I have to fill the blasted thing every day. To remedy this small dilemma, I stopped at Wal-Mart after church today. Here I stand in front of six different hummingbird feeders, some nice and some very basic. Which one do you think were made in China and which ones in the USA? Correct! The dull plastic feeders were made in the USA and the great looking ornamental ones in China. I did not buy a hummingbird feeder today. [1]

Now, here's a little of my history. I was born in a small town in Wisconsin. My family moved to Texas when I was very young. As a teenager, I lived in Minnesota. In 1995, I graduated high school and joined the United States Air Force. I served for 4 ½ years before getting out in 2000. After the cowardly 9/11 attacks, I voluntarily re-enlisted in to the Air Force and served another 3 years before getting out once and for all. To all the heroes who have the ability to make the military a lifelong career, I say Thank You! I currently work as a contractor. It's a lot like working for the government, but more responsibility and more pay. [2]

I live in New Mexico with my wonderful wife and daughter. We have two horses and a dog. We drive my Chevrolet Silverado, my wife's Toyota 4-Runner, and most often, I ride my Harley Davidson Heritage Softail. My hobbies are riding horses, spending time with my family, building things (anything), and home brewing. [3]

Enough about me; let's go back to Wal-Mart. We ended up buying some paint and a paintbrush this morning. The paint was made in the USA, but the brush was authentic Bangladesh or something like that. I did not have the option for an American-made paint brush at the Wal-Mart I went to.

Tomorrow, it's off to the hardware store for a new wall sconce... Wish me luck, because if it ain't USA made, I ain't getting' one!

Give America A Chance

August 2 Update

1. By the way, I did find a hummingbird feeder, but you'll read about that later.
2. I really do believe that if you served the military, you are a hero in my eyes and you will be a hero in my children's eyes if I have anything to say about it. If you can, or have, made the military a lifelong career, I genuinely and proudly say thank you. Just the other day, I went to a restaurant with my family and there was a military person in uniform sitting alone at the entrance. My wife walked over, extended her hand, and said "thank you for your service." You seriously deserve more credit than you receive. The military is tough, I don't care what branch you're in.
3. I no longer live in New Mexico. A couple years ago, I was forced to uproot my family and move to California to preserve my paycheck. I say forced, but obviously it was my decision. My career and the company that I work for, provides well for my family. I'm able to sustain my family with one paycheck… Something that's getting tougher and tougher to do. My wife is a stay-at-home mom with three kids now (we've gained a couple in the past few years). If you work for a company that provides for your necessities, you do owe them something. Jobs are tough to come by lately. And well-paying jobs are even tougher to find. Now I worked my butt off in order to get some college and the needed experience to earn my job, so if you're sitting on your butt expecting a higher paying job… YOU'RE DOING IT WRONG! You need to earn your paycheck. It's been said many times before that if you don't want to work, you don't deserve to eat. I agree. If you're unable to work because of whatever reason, that's a whole different story. That's where the benefits of being an American come to play. If you're able, but unwilling to work, and you want those same benefits, you and I have some issues.

August 3, 2009

I do not have a new wall sconce. Today was a busy day, but we (my wife, daughter, and I) still managed to make it to Lowe's and Home Depot. And I have to say that even if they had an ugly wall sconce that was made in the USA, I would have bought it. Zip, Zero, NADA… Not one. My daughter, however, had a great time rummaging through box after box shouting out "Ugh, this one's made in China too!" We did find some great American beef jerky, though…Yum! [1]

Today, however, I do not want to focus on sconces, but something far more important. Friends! You see, a couple months ago, I bought a home, hence the reason for re-furnishing. We have a great friend who we playfully refer to as our ranch hand. I provide the beer, my wife provides AWESOME cooking, and he provides my integral need for help.

Friendship is not something you can buy, and if you are, quit now and start over. I have always believed that if you allow a person to speak their mind, you have created a friend for life. I challenge you now. Find a person and open up a dialogue. Allow the other person to share what's on their mind… Just listen. Don't judge, don't even comment. Later, maybe later that day, week, or month, share something with them, and you've got a friend. [2]

Now all the manly men are saying, "I don't want to share my feelings." Fine, share your supper, share your beer, or share a project you need done. I never said share your feelings. I'm kind of the same way. I've got thick skin and not a whole lot bugs me, but I've got lots of work and fun projects that I want done around my ranch. I've also got a lot of old moving boxes that I will be sharing (giving away) to a friend tomorrow. [3]

Give America A Chance

So what does all this have to do with Giving America a Chance? We are all in America, land of the plenty. Does that mean I have plenty? No! Does that mean my friends have plenty? No! But between my friends and me, we have plenty! Find yourself a friend in need of something you have and share it. You will be rewarded tenfold. There's my challenge, my first challenge to you. Now Go! [4]

Man I love this country. God bless the USA!

August 3 Update

1. My daughter still likes to dig through items looking for the "Made in" label. I love it. I'm not going to reveal my wall sconce situation at this point (I have to leave some suspense), but you'll hear about it again and again… and again.

2. I got caught in my own little trick just the other day… There's a little back story to it that I'll share with you. Since moving to California, I found a great church for me and my family. We've gained some great friends and acquaintances. The other day, I met with the pastors (both friends outside of church as well). Right away, one of the pastors asked me to expand on some of my history… what did I always want to be when I was a kid, how would I describe myself in one paragraph… that sort of stuff. It's amazing how well this little trick works. I opened up like a book and, at the same time, I wanted to know the same thing about the other person!

3. Manly men… Man that is such a great phrase. When you think of a manly man, do you think of a lumberjack or a fireman? When your kids or wife think of that phrase, do they think of you? That question was meant to make you think…

4. Land of the plenty… Do you have a television? Do you have a cell phone? If you do, believe me, you have plenty. There are a lot of people in this country, not to mention this world, that would love to have what you have. I implore you to share what you have. Remember those people who are unable to work… Not unwilling, but unable. They might not have plenty. It's our job to help those people. You have been challenged. Will you accept?

August 4, 2009

Really, I don't have much to discuss today and since I'm in sort of a foul mood at the moment, I WILL RANT!

A few months ago, maybe a year, I needed a ladder. I went to my normal places: a couple hardware stores, Wal-Mart, and K-Mart. Not one USA made ladder. So, I had my choices... Mexico or China? Obviously, I chose Mexico. Really, does China have any interest whatsoever in keeping me safe? NO! Ten years ago, maybe... we were making them rich. But now, they remind me of a politician... they'll step on all the "little" people just to get themselves an inch higher. [1]

Remember back when there was salmonella in the dog food? Lead in children's toys? Ya, they want to keep me safe. Which reminds me, last week I went to a Pet Barn to get a water trough for the horses and while I was there, I decided to get a dog bone for my 11 year old lab. I bought her a Butcher's Bones ham bone that was made in the USA. The sales clerk had to point out the ones made in the USA because a majority of the dog treats were made in Mexico or (yes) China. Both countries that I'm sure care a great deal about my dogs' health. [2]

August 4 Update

1. I just read an article the other day that was talking about how China wants a "De-Americanized" world. The article was more about the frustrations toward our president than Americans in general, but as you read on, you'll notice that China has been planning something like this for decades.

2. This is the first of many times that I will mention a specific brand... Each of these brands are also listed individually on "The Raves" portion at GiveAmericaAChance.com. Now, just because these brands were made in America when I wrote about it doesn't mean that they still are. You still need to check the label. But having said that, when you come across one of these brands, please support their business. Write them a letter and tell them that you appreciate their efforts to support American workers (your neighbors).

As an aside, that 11 year old lab was the same dog that I mentioned in the beginning. She would have been 15 in just another week.

August 8, 2009

Yes, I'm fully aware that only 4 days into writing my book, I took three days off, but c'mon... seriously? Do you think I buy something every day? In case you actually need an answer to that, I don't. I did, however, buy something today. I've got rants from today. And, I've got a story from yesterday. Let's start chronologically according to my memory.

I got a phone call while at work yesterday from my wife. She was taking our daughter "back-to-school" shopping and wanted to know if I needed anything. I didn't, but I made the obvious request that she try to buy all-American. Duh! Long story short, when we were all home, my daughter wanted to show me everything she got and the "Made in..." label. [1]

Crayola... Made in USA! All of it... the crayons, markers, everything. Now, go out a buy Crayola. If not for you, than for your kids, nephews, nieces. Heck, get the neighbor's kids some crayons or something. Let's support these companies for all we've got. Elmer's glue, on the other hand, you've got to be careful with... Regular white glue, made in USA (very small print, though. What's up with that? Be proud!). Glue sticks... NOT! And none of the glue sticks were USA made. White loose-leaf paper... India? Mead spiral notebooks... USA! Whoo-hoo! Kleenex tissues, made in USA from domestic and imported materials? What exactly is the imported part and why did they have to import it? And from where? I'll have to call or write a letter to see if they'll tell me... Check back later. [2]

My wife also picked up coat hangers and saw a laundry basket that was made in the USA. The good stuff is out there... Seek and ye shall find! And when you do find, tell your family and friends... Heck, write a book. Brag about the good stuff. And if it's subpar to foreign made products, contact them and tell them you'd like to support them, but product "B" is better... What are they doing to improve their product? [3]

Now today, I went to a small feed store where I was half impressed and half discouraged. When I walked in, the clerk asked if they could help with anything. I said yes, "I would like a girth (for a horse) made in the USA." Well, she never checked to see if any were American-made. That's sad. I was, however, impressed to see that they had a used and consignment area in the store for saddles, bits, and the like. If you have a store, please don't be afraid to sell used items. Help out your fellow Americans... And while I'm on the subject, allow me to rant! [4]

Here we are, cruising down a 2-lane, 40mph road when we come up to a large farm tractor barely pushing 20mph. I realize that in the country, that's the common, easy way to get from place to place, but if there's a shoulder the size of a full lane, pull onto the shoulder and allow other cars to pass. It's just polite. This guy didn't. Nooooo, he weaved from side-to-side within his lane just enough to make it difficult for me to see around him. Had I not been pulling a trailer, I probably would've passed him on the shoulder. I typically don't get road-frustration, but a little respect goes a long way.

I also saw something very kind today. As I was pulling up to an ATM machine, a lady in the car in front of me pulled up, got an envelope, and immediately pulled out. I thought she was leaving, but no. She got back in the ATM line behind me presumably to allow me to get my cash and leave without waiting for her to fill out the envelope and do all her banking while I waited. Ma'am, I thank you. [5]

FYI... I still have not found a nice quality USA made wall sconce. [6]

Give America A Chance

August 8 Update

1. She still does this... I love it!
2. Not all Crayola products are made in the USA. Everything my daughter got for school was, though. We're still looking for chalk (sidewalk or otherwise) that is made in the USA. Crayola makes chalk, but not in the USA. They make it all in China. I will rant about that later.

    Now... What's Kleenex's secret? Turns out, it's not much of a secret. I decided to call the Kleenex customer service and ask what the imported materials used in their products consisted of. The representative on the other end of the line was very informative and told me that the pulp used to make the tissues was made of trees imported from Brazil. The domestic materials are made of post-consumer recycled product from the USA. And there you have it.
3. My apologies for not telling you at the time what brand the hangers were. They were Merrick hangers made in the USA. We still have them. Merrick Engineering makes all their plastic hangers at one of three plants in California, Texas, or West Virginia. I don't know the brand of the laundry basket. She didn't end up buying one, she was just checking.

    When I say to brag about the good stuff and write a book, I mean it. Tell me what you wrote, whether a blog or a published book, please tell me. I'd like to purchase a copy, as long as it's American-made, of course.

    And when I say to contact the companies, I mean that too. If you're wary about writing or calling a company, hit me up on the website and I'll either help you out or do it for you. Along with many other things, I want to make it extremely easy for you to encourage the companies you like to make their products in the USA... and make them better than everything else out there.
4. Consignment and re-sale stores are mentioned in detail a bit later, but I just want to touch on it a bit right now. Just because your store specialized in new merchandise doesn't mean you can't profit from used merchandise as well. Think about it this way. Let's say you make widgets. Some people want the latest and greatest widget that you make, and that's great. Some people can't afford the newest widget, but they'd still like one. Offer them a used widget. Not only will it allow your merchandise to reach a new customer base, but it will also prove that your widgets can stand the test of time. Would you buy a new gizmo if all last year's models were already broken? Think about it.
5. Talk about a slap in the face... Here I was still frustrated from the stupid tractor slowing me down a few minutes when a nice lady made those few minutes up for me. You've got to love it when you get things that you don't deserve.
6. Stupid sconce.

August 12, 2009

Well, it's been a few days, but have I got my hands on some great merchandise and even greater information.

Let me start with Glenn Beck. Yes, Glenn Beck, the radio and TV host. One thing I really like about Mr. Beck is the fact that if something bothers him or scares him, he questions it. I've heard him question President Bush many times as well as President Obama. But he did something the other day that blew me away... I will duplicate it right now. The phone number to the Senate switchboard is (202) 224-3121. The phone number to the White House switchboard is (202) 456-1414. If you don't like what your politician is doing, call them and tell them not to do it! If you like what they're doing, call them and tell them to stick to their guns. [1]

Now it's not like these are private phone numbers. You can find them all over online, but really, who looks? He blasted them all over Fox News and practically begged people to call. Good or bad, CALL! We are the only country in the world that has the ability to contact our elected representatives <u>and</u> be able to <u>expect</u> results!

I would also like to quote Mr. Beck once more just because I like the comment. "The survivor is the one who says, 'how will I get out if the engine catches on fire?'" Go ahead and dwell on that awhile. But also, be observant. Plan ahead. Find your escape. I pray you won't need it, but if you do... [2]

And now, as promised, some great products. There is a company called "Little Giant." They have saved me countless hours. They make a product called the "Trough-O-Matic™ Automatic Flow Valve." It is an automatic waterer for my horse trough. You see, I have three horses and only a 100 gallon trough. Both my wife and I work, so on a hot July day, I could come home to see only a few gallons remaining (hence the hours standing and filling). NO MORE! This has a simple design, looks alright, nothing to really break (except the rubber gaskets), and it works... Great! Best of all, made in the USA, with an American flag stamp and all. By the way, it was less than ten bucks. If you don't have horses, get one for your dog or something. I'll find out what else they make so you can be sure to get one of their products. [3]

I also got more paper products. Although you would think it should be the norm, I found something that shocked me yesterday... I went to buy envelopes, the good kind with the peel and stick so I don't have to lick 'em (especially if they're made in some foreign sweatshop... Could you imagine?) Anyway, the Mead brand envelopes were made in the USA! ROCK ON! Everybody go out and buy Mead products... Now! Here's the shocking part though... The generic equivalent was made in Malaysia. Oh well... I like quality which is why I chose to buy American products.

Well, since I bought envelopes, I also bought paper... Good paper. HP multi-use paper, for documents and pictures... Made in the USA! Thank you!!!

I have certainly bought, used, and seen more American-made products, but I think this is enough for now. But please, go buy something made in the USA. Support our country and its workers. Especially if you absolutely need something, check for the "made in" information... please... My 7-year old daughter wants to buy everything she sees if it has the Made in USA symbol or label and I can't afford everything... Help me! [4]

August 12 Update

1. Mr. Beck has a great website now linked to TheBlaze.com called the Marketplace. It's a website where Glenn Beck and his team pulled together and found small business products all made in the USA. It's certainly not a complete list of products, but it's one of the many sites out there dedicated to American-made products. Check it out. Not only are the products listed, but there's also a back story about the entrepreneurs behind the businesses.

   Now, to the meat of what I was discussing... Your elected leaders contact information... In this day and age, it's easy to get online and find the information you need to reach your Senator, Congressman, Governor, etc., but have you ever done it? Honestly, in my younger years, I count the number of times I wrote a letter or called an elected leader on one hand, and still have fingers to spare. That's not the right way to do it. These people work for you and they need to be reminded of that now and again. It's like this, if you asked one of your kids to wash the dishes, do you tell them one time and expect it done every single day as long as they live in your house? Doubtful. You tell them today and again tomorrow and again the next day. Why would you elect somebody that, quite honestly, you probably don't trust that much in the first place, to do what you elected him or her to do for the rest of their term? Remind them why you put them in that position of power. They are your employer. You hired them. You pay them.

   Don't start the "I didn't elect them" power trip (or cheap cop-out). YOUr state, YOUr country, YOUr community did hire them. And YOU do pay them. Now be accountable for them.

2. If you're reading this, you've already taken the first step in finding your fire escape. And men, I hold you to a higher accountability for the safety of your family; you'd better acknowledge and plan ahead for their safety at home, as well as their safety when you leave the house. Just as important, what's your first step in making sure your kids are safe in this country? Are you doing something about the political policies threatening you and your family? Call the people you elected and point them out.

3. I used this for years before I smashed it with a rock on accident. It got a bit too cold one night and I left the flow valve attached to the trough when the water froze over. My simplistic idea was to smash the ice with a rock to break the ice. After a few extra large rocks, I hit the flow valve and it was all over. I still recommend this product, just don't smash it with a rock and expect perfection.

   Little Giant is part of Miller Manufacturing Company which also makes Hot-Shot and Pet Lodge products. Their website sports the "Made in the USA" logo

and makes the claim that "98% of our farm and ranch products are designed, manufactured, and distributed in the U.S."
4. Proudly, my daughter still looks for the Made in USA label. Once you start, you won't be able to stop. You'll also start noticing that many of the rumors about American-made products simply aren't true. You don't have to compromise.

August 17, 2009

You may or may not remember, if and when this book gets published, that I am writing this during a pretty severe recession. I've had friends tell me that I should get the book written and published before there is no more USA. I say FAITH! Faith that my country will survive. Faith that my country will flourish. Faith that no single man, woman, or administration can bring my great country down! [1]

I do not want this book to be a book about politics. I would prefer that you, the reader, can't identify me as a democrat, republican, or other. If you absolutely need to know where I stand, know this… "I AM A RED-BLOODED, GOD-FEARING AMERICAN! [2]

Now back to my point… Recession. Earlier today, President Obama made a quote that I think holds more impact than he may have intended. If you were listening to Obama on August 17th, 2009 at 11:28 MST on CNN, then you heard him speaking to the VFW. He said, and I quote, "Cut the waste, save taxpayer dollars, support our troops." Wow! My entire book could be summed up in that philosophy. Here is what I got out of it:

1. Cut the waste – Buy American products. Less greenhouse gasses shipping to the US. Less money wasted on supporting foreign shipping. Buying directly from your neighbor who makes the product.
2. Save taxpayer dollars – Buy American products. No matter what administration is in power, you're going to get taxed… YOU. But will the company you are buying from help your country or another's? Keep your money and your taxes at home.
3. Support our troops – Buy American products and pray for our troops! Do you want our military soldiers, our heroes, to have the best equipment to keep themselves, foreign non-combatants, and this country safe? Keep your money right here.

August 17 Update

1. Well, it would appear that I was right. We made it through the recession and we'll break through the current government shutdown too. I believe in my country. I believe in the American people. I believe in you!
2. I love when I can quote others to get my point across. It tells me that I am not alone. It should tell you that you are not alone. I may have taken President Obama's words to a completely different level than he intended it, but the President's statement alone is pretty powerful.

August 23, 2009

Man, it's been a busy past couple of days. One of the only bad things about living on a small ranch is that the work is never done... Fortunately, it's a small ranch. And, the work allows me the ability to pass on products that work. American-made, of course. [1]

Before I started writing this book, I decided the house needed new toilets. My wife was all excited and proclaimed that we could buy Kohler toilets made in Kohler, Wisconsin. Awesome, I thought! Except it turns out this great "American" company makes their toilets in China (at least the ones available in southern New Mexico). So after an exasperated search, I found toilets made in the USA. Now that I've tested it for a couple months, I feel I can share the results. [2]

For those who care, this is a standard 1.6 gallon per flush (gpf) toilet. It has worked great. There's been a lot of issues with the low capacity models. Concerns that it takes two or three flushes to do the "job". Not the case here, my friend. I was able to clog it once, but it was on purpose. I tried a few times and it wasn't until I filled the toilet with almost half a roll of toilet paper did it clog up. I have now replaced every toilet in my house with Mansfield, Summit 3 toilets "Crafted in the USA." [3]

CAUTION—Not every Mansfield toilet is USA made. I don't know about all of them, especially the really expensive ones. I got the whole "toilet in a box" kit for about $150 at Sutherlands.

In order not to make this entire day about toilets, allow me to speak on something more "glamorous"... Socks.

After church this morning, the family and I headed down for grocery shopping at Sam's Club. Since we all needed new socks, we headed that way and found great

American socks for my wife and I. My daughter, on the other hand, was a bit more complex. We found some nice little pink, blue, and green socks made in Korea. When I say we needed socks, I mean we NEEDED socks! There's a company called "Zocks" that sells American-made socks through State Line Tack that we are going to get later on, but we needed them now. I asked my daughter if she wanted the Korean-made socks or could she wait until the order came in. She needed them now. I agreed to buy them... But wait... Over here, with a little more searching, there some un-colored socks made in the USA. She of course, chose the American socks. [4]

That's a lot of buildup, so here's the kicker... A patriot, a fellow shopper, came up and thanked us for explaining to her the difference at such a young age. I explained to her that we try to buy only American and thanked her for her acknowledgement. I am not alone! [5]

We filled our cart up with plenty of American-made food, supplies, and fresh produce. Also, I ran into a co-worker purchasing tons of food for an upcoming conference and had an American-made hand truck in his cart. The stuff is out there... It's everywhere... And, it's better!

August 23 Update

1. You know, I moved from one small ranch in New Mexico, to another in California… Apparently, I'm a glutton for punishment.
2. I know you're dying to hear about my toilet experiences. I'll get to that, but first, a couple things. First, I mentioned that I bought the toilets even before deciding to write my book… To answer a simple question, yes, I have long felt that American-made products are superior to foreign made products. I have long felt that American-made products can be found cheaper than foreign made products. I got sick and tired of hearing people say that it's too expensive to buy American-made products. I wanted to prove once and for all that it's not only cheaper many times, but it's also significantly better.
Some Kohler toilets are, in fact, made in USA. The ones that I found in my price range, however, were not. I don't know why or when they sold out, but until they come back home, I won't recommend them.
3. To clear up any confusion, the clog was made purposely by rolling out half a roll of toilet paper into the toilet after trying over and over with successively more and more toilet paper. It wasn't that I just happened to use half a roll to "finish the job."
4. I'll be honest… My daughter put more than two seconds of thought into the process. She's young and she likes the idea of having multi-colored socks better than plain ol' white socks. She made her decision without any input from me (other than my standard belief in American-made products). I am very proud of her for her decision. It took three seconds.
5. I have come across dozens of people over the years that have commented on my decision to buy American-made products. Then again, I'm quite vocal about it.

Give America A Chance

September 9, 2009

Of course I realize it's been a couple weeks since I've written. It's not my lack of concern, but rather my other commitments. And then there's a little bit of forgetfulness. You see, I have been tasked to write two employees' annual assessments. If they were two poor employees, or even just average employees, I probably wouldn't care much (if you're a poor employee, you should have a poor assessment and possibly employment elsewhere), but these employees are certainly worth my full attention. After completing the assessments came Labor Day weekend where the family and I hopped in the truck and drove across the country to camp and visit with family. I forgot my journal otherwise writing in the truck could have worked great. To be fair, however, we just got the Zocks we ordered today too. [1]

So now on to some company advertising. For my birthday last year, my wife and daughter bought me a Stenson Crushable cowboy hat. It's a thick, warm hat, but if you're as rough on hats as I am, it's worth it... Even in the summer. But this story isn't necessarily about my hat, but about my wife's new hat. While on vacation, we saw a similar Stenson Crushable cowboy hat in Brown, sized small—exactly what my wife had been looking for. After seeing my hat, she's wanted one of her own. The best part... Made in the USA! [2]

We have not had nearly as much luck with shoes, however. I have been looking for a comfortable pair of new tennis shoes and my wife wants something quick and comfortable to slip on. It's not that there aren't shoes made in the USA, because there are, I've just got to find them. When I do, I will let you know what I found.

There's a couple other things I need to discuss, but they'll have to come later. First let me talk about our president... He's right sometimes, you know... In a speech broadcast live to schools throughout the U.S., he told your children that if you drop out of school, you don't only fail yourself, you fail your country. I don't always agree with the man, but he makes good points now and again. Please remind your children of that if they're old enough to understand. This country gave them the opportunity for education. This country gave them the opportunity for health care (which is being discussed by Obama today as well—he's probably not right on this one). This country gave them the ability to choose their religion (speaking of which, I got a new Bible that I can't wait to tell you about). This country is great! And when I am dead, you will run it. Are you smart enough to keep it great? [3]

September 9 Update

1. I should add something to the "poor employee" bit. If you know you're a poor employee, then why are you? If you simply don't like what you're doing, secure something new and leave. If you're just lazy... Well, I have no sympathy for you when you lose your job.

    I need to mention real quickly that my daughter loved her Zocks. Because they stretch so much, it's doubtful that kids would really grow out of them. Chances are, like my daughter, they'll simply wear out after years of abuse. Not bad.

2. In case you're wondering, I still have this hat. It's a bit faded and worn down from sitting on the dashboard, but it's a great hat... My wife still has hers too.

3. Although I have tried to make this book as non-political as possible, I've realized more and more that there is no way to separate the fate of this nation from presidential policies. I stated a few years ago that President Obama was probably wrong on the health care issue. As the initiation process for "Obamacare" gets moving, it seems that there's more and more of it not moving. I can't complain too much, though. I'm not a fan of the whole deal. It's definitely not that I don't want people to have good health care; it's just that I believe in you. I believe in the people of this country. Despite what has happened over the past several years, I believe there is still much good in the hearts of the people in this country.

    Now I'm fully aware that I'm off topic for the conversation at hand, but I want to get some things off my chest. Let me tell you what I'm not a fan of. I am not a fan of laws that protect me from me. I am not a fan of laws that protect you from you either. See, it's simple. If we have free, universal health care for our entire nation, then we have to figure out a way to keep our nation safe. That means we'd have to limit when and how people drive (to avoid the dangerous times and places), what people eat, what people drink, and a plethora of other laws that simply shouldn't be.

    Would you rather eat, drink, fly, drive, and play as much as you want (so long as you didn't hurt anybody else) and have to pay for your consequences or be governed in everything you do and have the rest of the people pay for your consequences?

    So to tie it all in, what decisions will you make for the future of this country? What decisions will your children make for the future of this country? Will they subject themselves to rules and laws designed to protect themselves from themselves? Put simply, are you smart enough to keep this county great?

September 12, 2009

Now you may be thinking, isn't this a patriotic book? Why not write something on September 11th, Patriots Day?!? I'll get to that, but first... On a similar note to where I left off a couple days ago. I saw a quote today from Franklin D. Roosevelt. "We cannot always build the future for our youth, but we can build our youth for the future." I am left in awe of that statement... There are so many implications of that. What came to my mind is camping. I can't clean every natural campground in America, but I can clean up after myself and teach my kids to leave the environment better than how they got there... I can't control what our politicians do, especially when they discuss "the nuclear option" (pushing laws and bills that Americans don't want because they have the control). I can, however, help my kids grow up strong and teach them to be independent when they need to be and ask for help if necessary. [1]

OK, so why didn't I write on Patriots day? I usually do my writing at the end of the day and yesterday, I debated whether or not I should write. I debated what I would write if I was going to write something. I watched the speeches from Ground Zero, the Pentagon, and the field near Shanksville, PA. It all boiled down to this—I didn't want to. I remember September 11, 2001 very clearly. It was a horrible day. I've heard the conspiracy theories. I've heard the fears and the hopes. I chose to spend time with my family and friends who have served this country. I chose to remember in my own way and I won't push that on anybody. Period.

Today, however, I worked. I put up a new fence (yes, another one) and I used all-American products and tools, but I'll discuss those later. I still have not found a new wall sconce, though my active searching has stopped and I still need to tell you about my new Bible along with so many other stories. Later, though... I am tired. God bless!

September 12 Update

1. After all, this entire book is a call for help. I can't control how we build the future for our youth and I can't control how you build your youth for the future, but as a united country, we can control an awful lot. Not through laws, but by bringing out the good in all of us as a nation. I'll discuss this quite a bit more. Hang on, this isn't just a book about merchandise.

September 15, 2009

    What business does the president have butting in or even commenting on MTV awards? Is he the president of the United States or a kid hopped up on who gets an award? So if you remember today or yesterday, Kanye West did something you would expect a 3rd grader to do when his favorite girl didn't get picked to play with the red play-dough. I would've never heard about it except President Obama called Kanye a "jackass" during an interview. True, it was during an off-the-air segment and the reporter could've been more diplomatic about releasing it, but come on Obama... You were talking to a news reporter. Stick to the tele-prompter, you're not too good at this "thinking on the fly" stuff. I digress. [1]

    Onto something else... I made a false error about the fence I put up over the weekend. Unfortunately, some Chinese stuff slipped into my building materials. What I was doing was moving a chain link fence. The old metal posts were cemented into the ground, so instead of going without a fence for a while, I went to Lowe's and bought new fence posts which I was very happy to see were made in America.

    Also, I needed a new shovel or post hole digger. My last two Chinese shovels broke. Although I couldn't find an American-made post hole digger that I liked, I found an awesome shovel. A True Temper Excavator! American-made with a lifetime warranty. Anyway, I bought the shovel and posts, along with some concrete. [2]

    With the help of my wife and daughter, we lined up and put the posts in the ground. Then we took the old equipment from the old fence, the toppers and chain link, and moved them to the new fence. Here's the kicker... The toppers were all made in China. O'well, what's done is done. I'm not happy about it though. *can you hear my pouting?

Give America A Chance

By the way, I'm not telling everybody to go out and buy True Temper products... Quite a bit of their stuff was made elsewhere. Check the label! And tell the managers of the stores you like to shop at that you want American-made products. And check the label! [3]

September 15 Update

1. Not once, but twice. President Obama called Kanye West a jackass not once, but twice. I guess the guy really does hold true to what he says.
2. I've still got the Excavator. I used it to plant my garden here in northern California.
3. Granted, I go on quite a bit of rants in this book, but it's all about that last sentence. Check the label. I cannot put enough emphasis on the importance of American-made products. It's a great big loop. You start off by buying American-made products. Then, your friend, who is out of work, gets a job making American-made products. Later, your friend decides he can afford health care insurance. Your friend ends up a better position where he or she can buy more American-made products and the great big loop continues over and over.

Give America A Chance

September 21, 2009

Although I have much to tell, I want to talk about new Bible. A couple weeks ago, my family and I were at Barnes & Noble. We were just browsing when we heard some violin and cello players setting up to play. They were advertising the local symphony in a very effective manner. Maybe it was the music, but we got into the "buying mood" and began to shop more seriously. I came across The American Patriots Bible. Perfect, I thought... [1]

I bought it with great satisfaction. I truly enjoy reading different Bibles and I'm currently reading a NIV study Bible so it will be awhile before I sit down to read this one, but it has become my church-going Bible and there are lots of great comments, quotes, and editing. FYI... the full title is The American Patriots Bible – The Word of God and the Shaping of America. I will certainly be commenting out of it as I come across pertinent topics to my discussions, but let me start with a quote by Fischer Ames, the author of our First Amendment:

> Should not the Bible regain the place it once held as a schoolbook? Its morals are pure, its examples captivating and noble... In no book is there so good English, so pure and so elegant, and by teaching all the same book they will speak alike, and the Bible will justly remain the standard of language as well as faith.

Yes it should! Yes it is! This country was founded on the principles of God. Should not we, as Patriots, as free men and women, also base our patriotism on God and the Bible as well? [2]

The Rants and Raves of an American Patriot

September 21 Update

1. I need to be honest with you. I love this Bible. I love all the quotes and commentary written in the pages. I am sad to say that the quality is extremely subpar. Unfortunately, the pages fall out way too easily. Yes, I advocate for American-made products. Yes, I will be the first to tell you that I think American is better. But yes, I will be honest with you when I come across something that does not meet my expectations. Do I recommend this Bible? Yes and no. If you want a nice study Bible with some great quotes, get it. If you're looking for a quality, daily read Bible that will stand the test of time, this is not it.
2. Could you imagine a world where everybody learns the Ten Commandments, not as a list of taboo topics, but as a list of rules (not laws, at least not all of them) to follow for the better of all mankind. Just in case you don't know what they are, I'll list them for you in simple terms:
    1. Put God first in your life. Honestly, if you place God first in your life, is there a better role model?
    2. Don't make idols for yourself (including money). There are a lot of things that we focus our life on. But little things that we can't take to the grave with us are not something we should focus on.
    3. Don't use God's name in vain. Wouldn't the world be a relatively nice place if more people spoke more politely and cursed less?
    4. Work for six days and rest on the seventh. Too many times we feel like the weekend is ours. One of those days was designed as a work day. One of those days was designed as a full day of rest… Get some rest.
    5. Honor your father and your mother. I don't care the situation, HONOR THEM. Your father may have been a drunk or maybe you never even met him… Either way, love him and honor him. You don't have to be like him. Once, when I was acting like a rebellious teenager, my mom asked me a question that has stuck with me my whole life… "If you can't honor your earthly father, how can you honor your heavenly father?
    6. Don't murder. Murder is taking a life with malice and criminal intent. Killing, on the other hand is sometimes necessary.
    7. Don't commit adultery (or fornication for that matter). Don't look at pornography. Your wife should be the only one you lust after.
    8. Don't steal anything. This is pretty straightforward.
    9. Don't lie. If I could list the implications of lying, it would take another entire book in itself. Lying leads to a whole world of horrible

consequences. The truth can, and will, set you free (it's in the Bible). I'm not saying it's the easiest part of life, but you'll live a much freer life.

10. Don't covet what others have. This will lead to lying to get what you want, stealing to get more, and so much more. If there is something that you want (other than your neighbor's wife), work for it.

September 23, 2009

Here goes nothin'! Normally attacking a bank would, in my own opinion, ruin the chances of getting a book published… Well, here goes.

I saw something on Fox News today that made my blood boil. I mean it really ticked me off! The neighbor of a fallen hero went to line the street where the funeral procession was going to pass with American flags.

Awesome! I love those little flags. I lined the sand where my wife and I walked up to the pastor to get married with those little flags. But the patriot who tried to do this in her home town ran into a problem. Bank of America. If this was the only bad thing I've ever heard about Bank of America, I probably wouldn't have written about them, but I've heard way too many bad things about them to let this go.

This woman, who knew the fallen hero a good portion of his life, lined the streets only to have the manager at Bank of America rip out the flags after she placed them. The managers reason, it was against company policy and it could offend some people. WHAT??? Offend some people! Give me a break. What kind of customers are you worried about offending and do you really want them as customers? I encourage everybody right now… Go to your bank and if they're not flying an American flag, find a new bank! [1]

If you bank at Bank of America and they're flying Old Glory, great… If not, question them. If their policy forbids it, pull all your money out and write your local paper. Tell your local news station. Find a bank that isn't afraid of offending people offended by the American flag. And, go buy an American flag (made in America, of course) and fly it proudly from your home. Please fly the flag that represents your country and those willing to keep it great!

September 23 Update

1. Still, after these years, this story makes me upset. Not because it was a one-time story, but because stories like it are making headlines across the nation. Here's the deal put plainly. The American flag stands for much more than just you and me. It stands for more than just those who stood to protect it. Our American flag stands for valor, purity, and perseverance. Three things that I think this country needs now as much as any time in history.

   There's a whole host of rules regarding the use of our American flag. Some I agree with and some I don't. For example, the flag should not be used for advertising (United States Code, Title 36, Chapter 10, §176, paragraph i). I, for one, like seeing the flag on merchandise I want to buy; but it's against the "rules." On the other hand, there is certainly nothing against using it to honor a fallen hero.

September 27, 2009

Good gracious, I have got a lot to discuss and nowhere near enough time to discuss it. I should've written over the past few days, but alas, I did not... Normally, chronologically would help me remember, but I have to discuss the events from yesterday's trip... The Outlet Mall—dun dun dunnn.

We went with the purpose of finding a birthday present for my friend's 6-year old daughter and shoes for me and my family. I left with a sick feeling in my stomach.

Shoe store after shoe store. All of them made in China. I'll bet we hit nearly a dozen shoe stores and looked at hundreds of labels. I even went into one "quality" shoe store and after looking at a few, the sales clerk as if I needed anything. I told him that I wanted American-made shoes. In a snooty sort of tone, he informed me that all his shoes were European. After I informed him that every label I looked at said China, he quickly replied "well, they're produced in China." Sorry buddy, that's Asia... Wrong continent. We left. [1]

Then we saw the New Balance outlet store with signs hanging in the window: "Committed to the American Worker." Great! So, we checked it out.

We quickly came to find out that the whole commitment "to the American Worker" is only for one line of running shoe, the 993. This is when I started getting sick to my stomach. All these people running around shopping and not one that I saw was concerned with providing the Chinese our money. Of course I pointed it out to some people, but that didn't stop them. Apparently most people want what they want and they don't care how they get it. Sad! [2]

Birthday present. So we hit up the Disney Store. Keep in mind, this is a 6-year old girl whose birthday theme is "Tinkerbelle." After browsing labels, I asked the sales clerk if they had anything that was not made in China. After calling over the manager, the reply was (again sadly), I don't know.

We finally found her quality American-made products, but not at the Disney Store. We went with a neon coloring book, Tinkerbelle themed, and sculpting putty. We really tried to get sidewalk chalk, but every store we went to only had sidewalk chalk made in China. Seriously? The people in China wear masks to avoid the pollution and you want me to buy a dusty product (chalk) so my daughter and friends can breathe it in here in America? I don't think so. (3)

I also checked out a sunglasses store to see if I could get a good pair of American sunglasses. The store associate assured me that Oakley were USA made. When I found a good pair that I like, I double checked… "These are USA made, right?" Well, he said, the metal frames are contracted to Japan. WHAT?!? Give me a break! I don't have sunglasses—except a cheap pair of shooting sunglasses I wear for riding my motorcycle, Chinese made, purchased a long time ago. (4)

Onto something else. Last Friday night, my wife and I got a baby sitter and went on a date with another couple. We hit up a new Japanese steakhouse in the area. You know, the kind of place where they fling knives in the air and cook the food in front of you. I ordered a Kirin beer. My friend jokingly questioned why I didn't order an American beer. I told her that since we were at a Japanese restaurant, I wanted Japanese beer. Makes sense to me, but from the outside looking in, at a person writing a book/journal that is pro-American, it might be a bit tougher. I'm telling this story to let you in a little on my life. I don't disagree completely with foreign products, just upset about the quantity of products being outsourced to cheap labor – slaves. If you want European shoes, buy European shoes, not Chinese. If you want tea from Yemen, buy tea from Yemen… Or coffee from Columbia. Get the picture. If you don't, read on. (5)

In other news, Martha Stewart is ending her contract with K-Mart to dive into Home Depot. That will start January 2010. She wants to start producing outdoor furniture. I was never a fan of Martha Stewart products at K-Mart since most were not USA-made, but if she wants to do outdoor furniture, I know that there are a lot of furniture makers in the U.S. She said she has always liked tools and outdoor activities. She also noted that she will be active to ensure everything is of the highest quality. I hope she's right and she goes for American quality. When you see it, do me, yourself, and your country a favor… Check the label. (6)

Speaking of tools, a favorite topic of mine, I did some tool shopping of my own this weekend. Can somebody tell me where I can find some wood screws that are made in my country? Better yet, I'll do the research and get back to you. You demand them at your favorite tool store. I needed some ASAP, so I ended up with Made in Taiwan, Power Pro, all-purpose wood screws packaged in the USA. Not impressed. [7]

I hope by now you are feeling my anger, my frustrations, and my pity. The G20 Summit met earlier this week and they did what they do best… talk. Next week, next month, or year, will anything change? Probably not. Not if we as consumers won't change. They told China that they need to consume more and produce less. China is profiting from our current way of life. They won't change if we don't. If you haven't already, change NOW! Can I say it again? Check the label! Demand American-made products. I guarantee stores won't change for me, but they will change for us! [8]

Give America A Chance

September 27 Update

1. I've told this story to many people over the years and had the same humorous reaction every time. I understand being faithful to the product that you're selling, but c'mon, trying to tell me something is European because that's where it was designed just isn't the same thing. When my wife and I went to Hawaii awhile back, we wanted to bring home Hawaiian souvenirs. Many stores had products that were designed by a Hawaiian, but produced in other places. It's not the same. Some of the clothing was "designed" in Hawaii, but produced in California. To me, that's not Hawaiian.

2. So apparently, after some later searching, New Balance does make some other models in the USA, but within the other models, you have to search the labels. One particular pair of shoes, made in USA... Another pair of the same style and size... Not.

3. It's getting worse over there. Did you know that the Chinese recently "closed" an entire city due to the air quality (the city of Harbin with 11 million residents)? Unfortunately, I don't see it getting any better anytime soon. There has got to be a way to mass produce materials without clogging out our ability to breathe and raising the cost of production significantly. Would I pay an extra little bit to ensure a product is made in the USA and wasn't polluting our environment? You bet. Would you?

4. I still don't have a pair of sunglasses. It's not that I can't find all-American sunglasses; it's just that I don't want to pay a whole lot more for the privilege of wearing a logo. If you make sunglasses and you make them here in the good 'ol USA, please let me know. This is the type of item that shouldn't cost more than 10 or 15 bucks. I've been to plastic molding injection shops. You hand them a design and they can mass produce it by the thousands for extremely cheap. I don't need a unique stylish design, just something to keep the sun out of my eyes when I'm driving. Is that too much to ask?

5. This brings up an important point that I want to sidetrack on for a minute. My wife and I finally went on our first date in over a year. Kids will do that to you. We live far from family and we aren't the type of parents that are willing to hire a stranger to babysit. But, dating your spouse is important... Very important! Men, don't do what I did. Don't make your wife wait a year for a date with you. If you haven't been alone with your wife in the last 2 months, find somebody you trust to watch the kids and take your wife out!

   Now back to Japanese beer... You've no doubt heard the phrase "When in Rome, do as the Romans." There's actually a specific historical point of reference to the statement, but the whole idea behind it is politeness. It's also a rule that can be beneficial for you. Now my entire purpose of having a Japanese beer wasn't to be fully polite or because I may have been offending somebody by not doing it, it was just what made sense to me at the time. 99.9% of the time, though, I try to buy American-made products. That is something that is beneficial to me. Not only that, but it's just plain polite. By doing so, I'm employing my neighbors; I'm increasing the wealth of my country.

Besides that, the Japanese restaurant IS an American place of business and the employees ARE American. They may be of Japanese descent, but they're probably American just the same as you and me.

6. Turns out, quite a bit of the furniture is made in the USA. Unfortunately, it's quite expensive. The last bit of expensive furniture I bought was eaten by my dog, so I don't plan on getting some, but check it out if you're in the market. Just don't forget to check the label.

   Another interesting thing I found while checking out Martha Stewart products is that there is a Martha Stewart American-made market with events, contests, and showcases.

7. Carson Sales, GRABBER, Mutual Screw… There are actually quite a bit of manufacturers that make wood screws right here at home. Some even have explanations on why they make their products in the USA. So why doesn't every hardware store carry them? Because we're not demanding them… yet.

8. Look, I've already shown a dozen or more products that are made right here. One of the things that I found out during my year of documentation was that most everything you want can be found made in the USA (wall sconce's excluded). I've also found that most of the time, it's cheaper. There's still a whole lot of pages up ahead with a lot more products. The point is simple by now. Before the local stores change, we have got to change. Before the stores carry what we want, we have to tell them that we want it.

Give America A Chance

October 1, 2009

Holy Moly! Two months in and I haven't ticked myself off from recounting all of my daily frustrations. Believe me, I have other frustrations other than what I write, they're just not pertinent to making America a great home for my great-grandchildren (many, MANY years away).

Happy Birthday China! Who cares? Obviously the Empire State Building. In honor of the "People's Republic of China's" 60th Anniversary, the Empire State Building was lighted in Red and Yellow last night. It's so nice to see a piece of American history honoring communism – that's sarcasm! Not to worry though, a whole lot of people protested and wrote angry letters criticizing them. Good. Great! Now, all of you... Never go there again. Cut them off. Make a statement that if you support communism, you are not welcome in our country. [1]

Now that that's out of the way, I hear that Bank of America is cutting ties to A.C.O.R.N. pending an investigation. I'm not touching this topic with a ten-foot pole, but I recommend doing a historical search on the problems with A.C.O.R.N. Good for you Bank of America – now if you'll only start putting American flags on your buildings, you'll be off to a decent start.

Have you ever heard of an automaker called Fiskar Automotive? I hadn't until I heard that Uncle Sam is giving them a "loan" of 529 million dollars. That's $529,000,000!!! This is your money by the way. So, is this an American company? No. Are the workers American citizens? Nope. They're in Finland. We're sending our money to Finland. Why? To make an $89,000 "green" car. You can afford that right? Maybe get a couple? Ya, right!

Apparently, Bush W. started the program and AL Gore is continuing the backing. That's right, Al Gore's taking the lead on this now and pushed for this extra pocket change of ours for foreign workers. Let me make this simple... We (our country) are taking our money and sending it overseas to build another foreign car that only rich people can afford to buy. [2]

This isn't the only program of this sort... It's too bad we couldn't find an American willing to do this in our own country. Remember Jeep? A US contracting bid was put out to anybody who could make a vehicle for the military with specific standards (cost being one of them). Jeep has been through many owners, but it turned out pretty good. Why couldn't our government do something like that again instead of going behind our backs in order to slap us in the face! Yes, I'm angry!

On a separate, but equally important note, I went online looking for American-made wood screws. I wrote an e-mail to the ones who said "Made in the USA" and asked if they had any products Made in the USA. Pretty simple right? I've gotten one reply so far that said "Sorry, all of our products are made in China, but we are an American company." I'll keep you informed on the rest.

Now I'm good and angry! Good night and God Bless!

October 1 Update

1. I'm not trying to be a jerk here, but this really irks me. China is one of the top countries supporting slavery. I realize they hold an awful lot of our debt and we owe them, but that doesn't mean we have to celebrate them.

2. I could have deleted the preceding few paragraphs and completely denied that I ever wrote them, but I wanted to leave them in and include an apology. Fiskar Automotive is an American based automotive manufacturer. They are based somewhere in my current home state, California. I was wrong in my assumption that they aren't American based. That's about the only thing I was wrong about though. They did get a 529 million dollar loan from us and after a couple years, they're not doing too well. They've produced a bunch of cars out of Finland, but more recently, they've been laying off most of their workers, taking more loans, and laying off more workers.

This is where my apology ends. I was wrong about where the company was based, but I wasn't wrong about where the cars are produced or who can afford them.

October 8, 2009

Boy howdy! It seems the more I have to write about, the less time I have. Let me start with some products I bought today and we'll go from there.

I'm still on my hunt for wood screws (and a wall sconce, but I don't feel like going there). Today I checked out some screws that were, to me, unfamiliar. SPAX screws from Altenloh, Brinck, and Co., Inc. The other ones worked great, but these are made in USA or Germany (that's what the label says). Too bad I don't know which. I'll keep looking, though. [1]

I'm also plunging into a little more home plumbing, no pun intended. I need to re-route some copper water pipes. So I picked up a stretch of unidentified copper pipe and some 90 degree elbow joints made in USA. Whew, an American-made product! May I recommend NIBCO copper joints for your home? I also picked up a cheap BernzOmatic brass torch kit. Careful with this one, though. They had a lot of products made elsewhere, but if you check the label, they've got American-made products. The torch itself was clearly made in America, the propane was made in USA with global components. I asked the associate what that meant, but he didn't know and shamefully, he probably didn't care. Another letter I'll have to write… And I need to get on these letters. [2]

Enough of that, there's more stuff, but I'll get to those later. The moral of this story is… Check the label and ask for American-made products!

Here's a math problem for you… We currently have six million people filing unemployment right now. That's 6,000,000 people actively looking for work. China has 1.3 billion people and it's expected to grow 8% this year. Did you figure it out? Here's the answer, or at least part of it. We have 6 million people who want to work…

They want to do something and get paid for it. China has the largest potential market in the world. You figure the rest out. OK, I'll give you more answers. The United States is awesome at producing medical supplies. We're also awesome at producing vehicles, not to mention pretty much everything else we make. Now let's tap that HUGE market, put these people to work, and turn the tides a little bit. [3]

On the news the other day, I won't mention which broadcast. They said we depend on the Chinese to buy our bonds and treasury notes. Why do we depend on them? Because they make it and we buy it. I say change that! We shouldn't export our debt and import "junk"... We should export our merchandise and import what we need to be even. The president can't do it. I can't do it... Alone! But WE can! [4]

Here's another thing that bothers me. Hopefully it won't be a worry by the time this gets published, but General McChrystal, who was appointed by Obama, has requested more troops so we can win in Afghanistan. I didn't say continue fighting in Afghanistan, I said win! Any other word should not be in America's vocabulary. The defense secretary, congressmen, and senators are telling General McChrystal he should be more discreet. "Speak candidly, but discreet," they say. To me, that says secretly. And that ticks me off. Remember, war is supposed to be hell. It's supposed to be so bad that everybody, including our enemies pray for peace. I guarantee nobody prays for peace more than our heroes fighting for our homeland security and peace. Now... Fight for peace! Enough said. [5]

October 8 Update

1. A couple years ago, my neighbors invited me and my family for dinner. We were there for a few hours that evening. One of the things that sticks with me most was a workshop in his basement where he used to make all sorts of fun gadgets. There was a small homemade machine in the corner that he pointed out to me. Apparently, this "machine" was something he made for his kids. It was a real simple design with a great purpose. When his kids wanted spending money, he would send them down to the workshop where they could make a couple hundred or thousand "S" hooks. After a few hours, he would take them down to the hardware store and the kids would sell them to the storekeeper. How great is that?

2. I contacted the company that makes BernzOmatic torches and found that the "global components" may be a particular valve used in the manufacturing. The gentleman that I spoke with seemed shocked that the box actually mentioned global components since he thought everything was made in-house.

3. I realize that I didn't give many hints before asking for the answer, but I did that on purpose. If we want to turn this country around, we need to change the way we think. We need to look at a problem, 6 million people not working, one variable, 1.3 billion people in China, another variable, and start looking for solutions.

4. Does it bother you to have a country as big and as successful (at least historically) as ours and then hear that we depend on another country? It should.

5. Well, a few years after writing this chapter, we're still in Afghanistan. We still haven't won the war. I'm honestly not even sure if we could say were winning the battles. I feel extreme pity for our troops overseas. Our heroes are sitting away from home in a constant struggle for life and death, while our leadership plays petty games as if it's a chess game and American soldiers are simply pawns in a political battle. The way I see it is this: either Afghanistan is a threat to our homeland or allies, or it's not. If it's a threat, send our soldiers to win the battle and give them everything they need to do it quickly and easily. If there is no threat, bring our troops home.

    Additionally, does all the secrecy within this administration bother you as much as it does me? I don't need to know what our battle plan is, but I think that we, as American people, deserve to know whether or not our troops are provided with the best opportunity for success.

Give America A Chance

October 12, 2009

"We're going to treat them the way we would an opponent." I can think of a couple ways to treat this quote. Maybe if I was running for mayor or governor… Maybe even president. Being prior military, I could also attribute this to my commander speaking against Afghanistan, Iraq, or Iran. But for Anita Dunn, the White House Communications Director, to say this against an American organization, Fox News, on behalf of the Obama administration, is a disgrace! [1]

I often swap between CNN and FOX News channels believing the truth is somewhere in-between, but after this comment, I'll devote my time to Fox. C'mon President Obama… Show some class. Can you imagine if President Bush stated that he was going to treat any news organization, any American news organization, as an opponent? He would be crucified. [2] All this "opposition" because FOX questioned Obamacare.

The founding fathers of this great nation wanted to prevent the highest law of the land from creating new laws. And now, we have an administration that is trying to make a law so that every American must have health insurance… or be fined. You have to have auto insurance or your can't drive. You have to have homeowners insurance or you can't be financed to buy a house. Those are options. But you have to live! To be fined because you don't want insurance is a bit ridiculous. President Obama, I may or may not have voted for you. It's my right to keep that confidential still, isn't it? Or if I choose to support another candidate, am I your opponent as well? If an American or American news channel chooses to debate you, they shouldn't be labeled as an opponent. I digress, you choose! [3]

In other news, I've got a few American products to introduce. All of which I am very satisfied with. After all, I am an opponent to Chinese-made products. (sorry, that was a low blow).

In this paragraph, I am going to speak to a very small audience. If you don't have horses, feel free to continue to the next paragraph. You won't offend me. As a horse owner, I have to buy medical (vet) products for my horses. I've mentioned how good the American medical products are... The same goes for veterinary products. I picked out IVERCARE wormer for my horses this month for one reason... They put very clearly on the front of the package, "Made in the USA" with an American flag. I'm sure other wormers are made in the USA as well... Since I like to switch them up, if any others label it as well, I will mention it later.

My wonderful wife picked out a front door mat the other day. She got a MOHAWK Greenworks recycled rubber doormat. It is made of 100% recycled rubber—Great. It matches the décor of the house (they come in many colors)—Fantastic. It's made in the USA—Awesome! A quick note to MOHAWK Industries... Put that Made in the USA label proudly on the front label, don't hide it. [4]

One last quick product... Fiskars scissors. That's right, Made in the USA. I don't know about all their products, so check the label. [5]

Can I just say that I love this country? I love that I can offer different opinions. I love that I can argue with my president. I love that I can write out my feelings. I love the United States of America. Now, go out and buy products from the country you love. Hopefully, it's the same as mine. God Bless!

Give America A Chance

October 12 Update

1. Well, shortly after writing this, Anita Dunn left her position. Interestingly enough, she has moved on to being a contributor for some news agencies... Not FOX News, surprisingly.
2. I often wonder what would happen to other presidents if they would have said or done the same things as our current president. What would have happened if George Washington would have announced that he was going to win a war by declaring he wanted to win the "hearts and minds" of the enemy? Think about it. When a current president does something, anything... Think about what the repercussions would have been had that president done the same thing a hundred years ago? Just a thought.
3. OK, I went on a tangent on that paragraph... I included a few different things so let me clarify now that I've thought about it and actually read it as one paragraph. In 2009, I was upset about the idea being forced to pay for health insurance just because I wanted to be an American. A few years later, I'm livid! My fears from 2009 have come to pass. For those that wondered whether I actually wrote this back in 2009 or added it later to make my point, I would offer you to stop by my place and view the actual journal I hand wrote it in. I knew Obamacare would be a disgrace to the country in 2009. I see now that I was definitely correct!

    Then, I shot a jab at President Obama concerning whether or not I was your opponent because I disagree with you and write things that don't always paint you in a perfect light... I've done the same thing to his predecessors. It's not that I don't like the individuals personally (I've never met any of them), it's just that I wonder how they view me when I disagree with them. As an opponent... a challenger? President Obama (and all previous presidents for that matter), I'm not competing against you. I've never even run for president. I simply disagree with some of the things you stand for. If you want my vote, don't try to compete against me, convince me!
4. I love it when companies proudly display that Made in USA label. I would encourage every company that makes American-made products to proudly display your label... Put my favorite three words right on the front of the package.
5. Still have these scissors too. Nice pair of scissors.

October 14, 2009

Often times, I write little notes throughout the day on topics I hear on the news or conversations I have, or ideas as I think of. Then, at the end of the day, I compile them into my "book." Every so often, I forget the paper when I come out to write, but I still try to touch on the important topics. So what's the point? A while ago, I wrote this on a note: "If you surround yourself with people who are only there to back you up, for the purpose of encouraging others to join you, are you really encouraging or bullying?"

OK. Still, so what? Well, let me tie that with more recent events. President Obama held a conference with a room full of hand-selected doctors to advertise his health care plan (which hadn't been written at this point). Obviously, they were doctors that wouldn't question the president. [1]

Then, if you remember earlier, then-Senator Obama spoke about how he would like a government health care system. Senator Grassley mentioned that we're on a slippery slope to a government health care system. The unions, who don't currently like the idea, have been asked not to go public with their criticism (more secrecy). [2]

I really don't want to get into politics, but this really bugs me as an American. Why all the secrecy and back talk? Why not just come out and say what you want and let Americans vote on it. Why is the senate voting (and passing, I might add) on bills that haven't been written and are not publicly available? Why are the bills written so that the average American can't understand it? Is this what you think America wants? If you keep pushing, senators... If you keep pushing, congressmen... If you keep pushing, President Obama, we will push back. Americans have the right to protect this nation and the freedoms that make it great. You can't secretly take away our right to vote or choose who we elect. Listen to the citizens of the United States of America, not your own agenda. You were elected because we voiced out for change. Our change is not your change. Enough! Now, I'm angry! Stop the bullying. Stop the secrecy. If you can't encourage us to accept your offer, you can't force it. We're smarter and stronger than that. Never underestimate the power of America! [3]

October 14 Update

1. This isn't anything real new. Although it bothers me, many presidents only speak in front of a hand-selected audience. I think it's cowardly to only encourage those who agree with you. It's easy to stand strong with those who agree with you. I realize it's natural for us to surround ourselves with like-minded people, but when you're trying to sell something, I find it silly to try to "sell" our ideas to those who already have our ideas. If you want to sell your idea, you have to talk to those who completely disagree with you. Not only will you have the opportunity to actually change people's mind, but you'll also have the opportunity to learn something. Just once, I would love to see a leader stand in front of a group of people and truly work to persuade others to accept their idea. Does it seem odd to you that our leaders seem afraid to publicly argue their positions? Even in presidential debates, arguments are often vague enough so that every statement, when viewed alone, is something that pretty much everybody can agree on.
2. Essentially, you're taking a group of people who disagree with you and asking them not to tell anybody that they disagree with you. The only way that's going to work is if they have something to gain by not publicly disagreeing with you. Think about it… What are the unions gaining by not speaking up?
3. I would love to see our government pass a bill that mandated a waiting period between publicly releasing a bill and voting on it. Something along the lines of one day per page of the bill. If you write a 1,000-page bill, you have to wait 1,000 days from the time you release it before it can be voted on. If you have an idea that is so important, so pertinent to today's environment, then write a bill that speaks to it directly and vote on it. When a congressman or senator writes a bill that takes up thousands of pages, how much of that is "fluff?" How much of that has a hidden agenda in the fine print?

    When the health care debate was going on a while ago (President Bush was in office), there was an agreement that health care should be able to cross state lines. Then some of the politicians came out saying that it was a start, but it wouldn't be enough to fix our health care system. My thinking is that if everybody agrees, then write a bill that passes that kind of legislation. Something like this… "Health care systems and providers will not be limited by state lines." Done! Do you want to pass it or not? Now we'll start working on another simple step on our way to a solution. Why does the political version of the same thing have to take up hundreds or thousands of pages? Remember, every journey starts with a single step.

Give America A Chance

October 21, 2009

OK, so it's been a week since I've written. But if I could make the beeping sound in your head like the old genuinely important news bulletins of the past, I would. Part of this past week has been contemplating and partially frustrating. I submit to you now that it is impossible to write a book with the intention of awakening a nation without getting both political and religious.

> We establish no religion in this country, nor will we ever. We command no worship. We mandate no belief. But we poison our society when we remove its theological underpinnings. We court corruption when we leave it bereft of belief. All are free to believe or not believe; all are free to practice a faith or not. But those who believe must be free to speak and act on their belief, to apply moral teaching to public question.
>
> I submit to you that the tolerant society is open to and encouraging of all religions. And this does not weaken us; it strengthens us…
>
> Without God, there is no virtue, because there's no prompting of conscience. Without God, were mired in the material, that flat world that tells us only what the senses perceive. Without God, there is a coarsening of the society. And without God, democracy will not and cannot long endure. If we ever forget that were One Nation under God, then we will be a nation gone under.
>
> -Ronald Reagan

Thank you sir! I could never have written so eloquent a speech to speak the words on my mind to the Spirit in my heart. [1]

I bring up religion again, because it is such an important part of my life. God is the reason I can consider myself a good man. Not good by God's standards, although I have a personal savior who will someday present me before God as good, but good in the world's standards. [2]

I'm not a drunk, a drug addict, thief, murderer, or rapist. I honestly put forth a very strong effort to never lie (though I am imperfect). I don't mock the humble or tease the poor. Do you know why? It's because of God. If there were no higher power, no after life, to answer to, I wouldn't care. If I weren't anxiously waiting my eternal life in heaven, I would steal, drink, and party till the cows come home. I try to be good; however, so I can help others accept the reward I have promised to me. I can't earn my way into heaven any more than you can earn a birthday gift from me to you. I can offer and you have the option to accept. [3]

I'm way off track, but I'll continue so I don't pass the wrong intention. If you accept the gift of a savior to stand between you and God to present you as perfect, you will want that for everybody you care about. With that gift comes the responsibility not to abuse the gift… But more than a responsibility is the weighing on your heart to do good for those you care about. It's the weighing, the "prompting of the conscience" that guides us.

All right, now that I've gone on a bunny trail an elephant could follow, let me get right to the point. DO good things! Let me jump to another quote:

> The choice before us is plain: Christ or chaos, conviction or compromise, discipline or disintegration. I am rather tired of hearing about our rights and privileges as American citizens. The time is come—it is now—when we ought to hear about the duties and responsibilities of our citizenship. America's future depends upon her accepting and demonstrating God's government.
>
> -Peter Marshall

Do you agree with that? Are you sick and tired about people saying it's their right to have health care when they do nothing to promote the future of America? Are you sick of hearing the wealthy talk about their "privileged" problems that we "little people" wouldn't understand? Or when the prominent get away with criminal actions? … Senator?

We have a duty to this country. We owe a debt to this nation. America, your country depends 100% on you!

Give America A Chance

Let me loop this all back around... We should want to do good for the sake of our country and those we care about. How do we do that? Support your country. It doesn't always have to be "buy American products." Maybe you could donate an American product to train an American product. What? Are you a product of America? Did you graduate from an American school, learn a trade in America, or acquire a hobby from the freedoms of America? You are an American product. So what have you done for your country besides buy American "stuff?" You can easily "purchase" American products by donating yourself, your time, your money, and your stuff.

Give your old clothes to the single mother down the street with five children. Can you help the elderly neighbor repair his fence? What about hire those five children to mow your lawn or pull weeds? Can you bake a dozen cookies for the local homeless shelter? Are you so booked with time that you can't get your waitresses name at your local American diner and pray for her and the extra tip you gave her to get her through school? Or are you on a rampage to get through life and "disintegrate" this nation?

You're reading this book, so I already know your answer. You are a Patriot of this country. You are a good person in the world's eyes. Don't feel guilty because you haven't done enough. Just... Do your best! Now go be an American like your country depends on you... Because it does. God bless America! [4]

October 21 Update

1. "You are free to believe or not believe…" That quote is amazing. There are many countries that simply don't have that same freedom. Not only can you choose to believe or not to believe, but if you choose to believe, you can choose to whom you believe in.
2. I want to be clear… The last thing I want to do is puff my chest out and say, "Look how good I am". I am not bragging. It simply comes down to worldly eyes. In the world, many people look at somebody and say, "That is a good person," or "stay away from that person, he's a bad man." I would like to think that I am a good person based on the next paragraph…
3. Quite honestly, if I weren't a Christian, I wouldn't see much reason to be a "good" person. I know that there are many of "good" people who don't have a higher faith. My question for those people is why? Why do you choose to be "good"? I would venture a guess that there is a significant reason other than I don't want to be a "bad" person. If you're reading this and can answer, e-mail me and let me know… Life is always about the lessons you learn and I want to learn!
4. I didn't want to interrupt the original tangent from a few years ago with current tangents, so I decided to just add a little after the past few paragraphs. It seems that in the past years, we've been hit with so many motto's that lead to the same thing… "Just do it." "Git 'er done." I'm honestly not sure what message the others are pressing, but I hope I've made my point clear. This is your country! This is your home! Take care of it. Treat it right. Help those who genuinely want and need help. You're generosity will be paid back. Trust me.

Give America A Chance

October 26, 2009

Halloween is just around the corner and my wife and I are having a small Halloween party. Last year's theme was children's story book characters. The goal was to dress like a storybook character and bring the book to be donated to a local bookstore that gives a free book to every child that walks in. [1]

This year is different... Easier, but much harder for me. The theme is Toys for Tots. Dress as a child's toy and bring the toy for a donation to Toys for Tots. Easy enough, right? Try finding a toy for your character Made in USA. I am going to be one of those little green army men. Most of the modern versions you find are made in other than the USA. I sent an e-mail to TimMee Toys trying to figure out if all their products are Made in the USA and where I can get them—I'll let you know when and if I get a reply. We also ordered stuff online for my wife's and daughter's costume... I'll fill you in on the quality when we get it. [2]

Another problem we had over the past few weeks was trying to find children's coats to donate to our church. I could not find on affordable coat made in the USA. After a long discussion, my wife finally bought some foreign coats. Her reasoning was that it was better to give a coat to a child who needs it and not worry about where it was made. I partly agree.

You see, I've got this crazy idea that if we demand products made here, people will have to make them. If enough people are needed to make them, the unemployed will be able to find a job. If more people are working then more people are paying federal taxes. If more people pay their share, the less taxes the rest of the labor force will have to pay. And, if those recently employed people buy products made here, the more products will have to be made. The cycle continues. Am I crazy or is this basic economics?

Do you understand what I am saying? More American workers equal more American products. More American products equal more American workers. More American workers equal more taxpayers. More taxpayers equal less individual taxes!

What I don't want, however, are laws forcing us to buy American products. I want us, you and me, to choose to what is best for our country. If you've been reading this, hopefully you're seeing how everything is tying together. Quite simply, what I've been saying again and again is that we are the determining factor for the success of this great nation. Let's make it great! Now go do something great!

October 26 Update

1. That party was a lot of fun. I was Paul Bunyan. Easy costume… just a flannel shirt, boots, and some time to grow my beard. I even put my dog in a blue shirt so she could be Babe the blue ox. My wife was the paper bag princess and my daughter was Junie B.—a great set of books for kids. On the inside cover, they have "Manufactured in the United States of America" proudly printed on the copyright page.
2. I never got a reply from TimMee Toys, but I found out that the army men toys aren't made in USA, so I guess that's my answer. I ended up buying some older TimMee plastic army men that were made in USA from EBay.

    Since I told you last year's costumes for everybody, I'll tell you this years as well. My wife was a doctor. Unfortunately, I forgot the toy doctor kit that we picked up, but it was made in USA. My daughter wore a Cowgirl Kate and Cocoa outfit (a horse costume my mom made). She donated a stuffed horse made in USA. More on that later.

October 28, 2009

I'm not going to get on my high horse today. I've got a couple "praiseworthy" mentions, though.

A couple days ago, my "service engine soon" light came on for the first time on my 2002 Chevrolet. Not bad considering I've put more than 165,000 miles on it. I took it up to Pep Boys auto repair shop and they came out with their diagnostic tool and found a 440 error. Turns out there was a vacuum hose for the fuel injection that was sucking and leaking gasoline over the engine. They didn't have a replacement part, but I was able to get Magic Mounts hose repair tape (made in USA) and Dorman HELP quick connect hose clamps (made in USA). With a little creativity, I fixed the problem and drove away only $4.00 poorer. You can't beat that. By the way, one of the Chevrolet dealerships wanted almost 90 bucks just to run the diagnostics on it. [1]

Also, for some crazy reason, it started snowing out here in the desert today (global warming?). With the chill and snow, we decided to get out the horse blankets, but we were one short. We headed to our local Horse and Hound looking for another blanket, but they were all made in China. The sales associate made a call to a competing store and found some made in USA for me. We ended up getting a great deal on an Abetta horse blanket, of course, made in USA! [2]

Kudos to Pep Boys and Horse and Hound for excellent customer service and the American-made products we were able to find. They all come with my highest recommendation! That's what makes this country great... Thank you.

October 28 Update

1. I have to tell you that I continued driving that truck with this fix for the next 30,000 plus miles before I sold it. The products really worked that long.
2. In the movie, Miracle on 34th Street, Santa gets in a bit of temporary trouble for sending customers to competing stores so they could get what they want. Later, it turns out that it's the best thing to happen to the store. I only mentioned Horse and Hound in this article since they were the ones that made the call for me. They also came up with the idea. Great customer service is something that seems to be fading away. Whenever you find great customer service, tell others… We all appreciate it!

October 30, 2009

Have you ever had one of those times when you've publicly announced "I would never," or "If I was in that situation, I would..."? Remember last week when my wife and I had the discussion about buying foreign made coats to donate to children in need. My wife was intent on saying that it's better to support the children than worry about where the coats are made.

And remember how I mentioned that it got cold and snowy here over the past couple days? Well... I was put to the test in my own life and the warmth of my own family.

Upon turning on the heater in my home, I blew a specialty fuse that cannot be bought at any hardware store on planet earth. I have a pellet stove that we have used occasionally and a wood stove that I have never tested. So I went on the hunt for a couple electric heaters. Do I buy a Chinese heater that probably works just fine or put my family at risk lighting the wood stove? By the way, my house was 40degrees inside. What would you do? In my mind, both were fairly risky. [1]

I could not bring myself to buy Chinese merchandise. Instead, I chose a couple extra fire extinguishers, low soot producing fire logs, and smoke/CO2 detectors. My house is warm, my family is safe, and I don't have the gut wrenching feeling that I just supported China. I'll get the heater fixed soon. [2]

Additionally, Lowes had some fairly cheap bags of pellet stove fuel, but it didn't have where it was made written on it. I called the Forest Energy Corporation immediately and asked where their products were made. The lady on the other end assured me that they were made in Show Low, Arizona so I bought 200 lbs. [3]

Oh, I also got a couple packages yesterday for my Toys for Tots Halloween costume. The TimMee army soldiers I bought on EBay came with a hand-written note from the previous owner—who was obviously a collector. He apologized that one of the army men (the radio operator) had a broken antenna and sent two additional radio operators with extra-long antennas, though they were a slightly different shade of green. He also wrote that they were probably produced in the 1950's or 1960's. I had a fleeting thought to keep them for myself and buy cheaper ones for donating, but I won't. I hope some child has a blast with them. I know I would have in my childhood. (4)

Additionally, my daughter's stuffed horse arrived. The label read:
> Stuffington Bear Factory is one of the last remaining factories in the United States. Thanks for making one of our animals part of your family.

It's sad to see that so many of our children's products are made in countries other than here, but I'm glad they're so proud of their products. Check them out and get a couple for your kids (while you still can). (5)

That's it for today. Keep on in your pursuit to find quality American-made products. Thank you for being a patriot. God Bless!

October 30 Update

1. Just to clarify... I don't think buying heaters is risky. The risky part is some guy trying to buy all American products and selling out by voluntarily buying Chinese made products.
2. The fire extinguishers, fire logs, and detectors were all made in USA, but I can't remember what brand they are now. I apologize for forgetting to clip the label and mention them.
3. In all fairness, I used my Chinese-made cell phone with Japanese made battery to look up and call the company. Unfortunately, I don't know what I can do about that. Throughout the winter, I probably purchased about 2 more tons worth of wood pellets. They worked very well. I also finally got out on the roof and cleaned out the chimney on my wood stove to make it safe as well.
4. So, I've been back to the TimMee website over and over. As far as I can tell, all their products are made in USA, but since I couldn't see the individual package, I thought I would be taking a chance. Check them out and see for yourself.
5. If you're ever in the Phoenix, AZ area, check out the Stuffington Bear Factory. Their stuffed animals are still made in USA and they give free tours.

    I saw a website the other day that was discussing the levels of lead in Chinese made toys. Some of them were thousands of times over the legal limit. Of course, somehow they get away with it. I'm telling you, you don't want your kids playing with a lot of this stuff. There were quite a bit of comments mentioning the same thing. There are millions of patriots in this country and you are one of them. Let's get more on our side, America's side, and set this nation straight.

Give America A Chance

November 3, 2009

Today, I'm feeling extra patriotic. It all started with an eye-doctor's appointment earlier in the week. Without going into detail, the doctor told me that I needed to wear sunglasses. If you've ever looked for sunglasses made in USA, you know it's pretty tough. Off the top of my head, I can think of only one, OAKLEY. I checked them out and, no offense to OAKLEY (you make great sunglasses); I can't spend $200 on something I will scratch or lose in a few months. I found a website that makes sunglasses in the USA and models their design off the expensive brands Made in Taiwan and Japan (and, of course, China). I may look at those, but that's not why I'm feeling patriotic. [1]

On the way from work to glasses shopping, I was listening to "The Great One" on the radio. If you don't know who that is, I highly encourage to look him up… I could tell you his name, but that would be too easy—besides, I'm sure he'll come up again and if I do, I'll mention him by name. For now, let me say that he is a great patriot. The kind that believes in America and Americans as individuals.

So he was talking about the elections that took place today in New Jersey, New York, and California. His primary concern was getting people out to vote. He's the kind of man that sends chills down your back because you get so fired up to protect this great nation—or makes you feel shamed because you didn't do what so many people died to give you the right to do. We take it for granted now… voting. And did you vote? I hope so. Nothing can make you feel more like and American than choosing your leaders and your laws.

But even more than that, as my wife and I were at the sunglasses store and my wife got on her soap box. Have you ever heard a strong woman speak on the liberties and freedoms of America? I didn't ask my wife to join me on my quest to buy American products. She did it on her own. She now does it without even thinking... She even corrects me sometimes. My wonderful wife stood by my side and told the sales clerk that "buying only American products started out as a project, but has now become our quest". OUR quest!!! She's often stood by me as I tried to buy American-made products, but she never declared it as her quest as well.

Men, if you're blessed to have a woman stand by your side, you better treat her right. You better honor her and lift her on a pedestal. And, if you're a man, not a boy, but a genuine MAN, you better lead your family in every right way. If you do that, and do it correctly, she will join you; she'll join your quest in life. You won't even have to ask.

That is why I feel especially patriotic today. Today was a great day to be an American. And tomorrow? Tomorrow will be better because of it. [2]

November 3 Update

1. I discussed a bit about OAKLEY back in September too. I honestly have nothing against the company other than their prices. I'd like to see them make a disposable brand for people like me who aren't used to wearing sunglasses and often take them off so I can "see" and then lose them or end up crushing them somehow. Trust me, I have done that before and I will do it again.
2. My wife is still standing by my side... In fact, I was playing some stupid game on my phone the other day and she asked if I was killing monsters. I told her that she need not worry; I was killing all the monsters. She told me that "she never worries when she's with me". How awesome is that! Man I love that woman!

November 11, 2009

Happy Veterans Day! I would like to express a very genuine and very sincere thank you to every veteran, active duty service member, police officer, and public servant out there. You are what holds this country together. I certainly don't want to exclude any other patriots, but these people are to you and your family what the secret service is to the president... They are the ones jumping in front of the bullet for you. So again, I say thank you!

Well, the other day, I mentioned looking at sunglasses made in USA online. I ordered a set (they came by the dozen for around $60. When the package arrived, I quickly opened it and my wife, daughter, and I each grabbed a pair, ripped off the tag, and threw them onto our heads. They felt good, they looked good. I was pleased with my purchase. But then...

Let me backtrack a few minutes. I mentioned that we ripped off the tags, but we left the little stickers they put on the lenses because, well, they had an American flag on them and we were in a rush. The lens sticker proudly stated "polarized lens made in USA". The tag that we ripped off in our haste said "made in China". Apparently, only the lens is American-made, but the plastic frames were made in China. All in all, I consider it a bust and I will not promote the company or the product. [1]

On the other hand, I did get an American-made product that I am extremely happy with. Here's a little story.

My parents are coming to visit me this weekend. It will be the first time they've both come since I got married. Now, they don't expect me to do anything special for them which is why my family and I will spend the next few days frantically cleaning and preparing our home for this special visit. Normally, I would surrender the master bedroom for honored guests, but there's no guarantee they would accept. The other option is the guest room with a not-so-comfortable futon. Or they could stay in the 5th wheel they are bringing down, but I'm not going to say come visit, but don't go in my house.

Our options were clear; we have to get a more comfortable futon if that is what they choose. And believe it or not, we found a comfortable futon mattress... for 600 bucks! Mom, Dad, I love you, but we gotta eat, so no!

So we checked Target. In their HOME line, they have a 2" memory foam topper that is much more affordable, and... You guessed it. It is made in USA. So if your bed sinks and needs an upgrade, check it out. It is Awesome! And it comes with a 7-year warranty. [2]

Nothing else to report at this time. Stay true to your country. Support your troops. Honor your veterans. By the way, my dad is a Vietnam veteran. Thank you! I love you dearly.

November 11 Update
1. One dozen sunglasses lasted me about a year before they were all lost, destroyed, or damaged beyond use. Do you see why I won't buy an expensive pair of Oakley's?
2. That mattress lasted us a couple years until we got a new puppy that thought it was a chew toy and destroyed it. I don't think that is covered in the warranty—I didn't even try.

Give America A Chance

November 17, 2009

My folks came and went already, but they'll be back for Christmas so that ought to be fun. Sunday at church, the pastor asked for all veterans to stand and be recognized. It was the first time I was able to stand up next to my father and be recognized for that sort of thing. I've sat by while he had been recognized in the past, very proudly I might add. And he's been by my side through many of my Boy Scout awards and my Eagle Scout promotion… He was even there when I graduated basic training—my mother was also there and even my sister showed up in uniform (she was Air Force too), but this was the first time I got to stand next to my father on Veterans Day. [1]

OK, enough of the sentimental stuff… Let's get to the stuff we fought (and are still fighting for). We owe more than 790 billion dollars to China. That's $790,000,000,000.00! And that's just to one country. We have plenty of other credit cards with huge balances on them. I say we, because that's what it boils down to. Not this country, not the government. But our country, our government… We! [2]

Allow me a second to ask you some personal questions. Are you in debt personally? Do you owe on a house, car, loans, credit cards? How much of that debt do you want to force upon your children? Any good parent would like to say "none." In fact, you'd probably like to leave them with plenty of assets… debt free! Why should we as a nation be any different?

Many people have quoted a line that originates out of some great speaker, and I don't know who, but "A setback is a set up for a comeback!" Good line, eh? We've been set back so far, we have an awesome opportunity for an awesome comeback.

You know my idea on how to get out of debt… Buy American products. Heck, we got into this debt by buying foreign products. We bought stuff and sent our money to them. We stopped buying our stuff. We stopped sending our money to us.

If Toyota and Kia can assemble vehicles in the USA, why can't GM, Dodge, and Ford? Why do I own a Chevrolet truck assembled in Canada? I don't understand that concept. If other companies can produce cars here, why do I constantly hear that it's too expensive for American manufacturers to produce here? I don't believe it and I don't accept their excuses. The time for us to demand American workers and American products is now. We need to demand products to be produced here and exported there via an American company.

Am I saying create laws to prohibit foreign alternatives, NO way! I'm saying that we as consumers need to demand American products or we don't want what they supply. They key to my alternative solution is for the government to step aside and let the Americans decide what is best. [3]

It's not OK for us to say drilling for oil is bad and at the same time buy from the Middle East. We should be using our own oil while demanding the oil companies find alternative solutions. If one American oil company agrees, we boycott the others until they decide to play our game. That's the power of 300,000,000 angry Americans. [4]

You have the right to pursue happiness, not the right to live fat and happy on the government's dime. The government is not here to make that pursuit for you. Right now, some 15 million people in this country are jobless. That means they depend on you to give them a paycheck. Most of those genuinely want to work. Sure, there are the slobs who don't want to, but that's the minority. We have to power to give them work, but we have to want what they're working for. Scratch that, we have to DEMAND what they're working for.

There are a lot of great American companies making products right here in our backyard. Together, we can make them grow. We can force them from their garage operations into mass producing facilities. We can make Americans rich. Rich Americans pay a lot of taxes and employ a lot of people. Have you ever worked for a poor person?

I'm sure I'm making a lot of people upset with my words, but this is my conquest. This is a fight I've chosen to step in to. I want my children to inherit great wealth. I want my country to have great wealth. I want every American who wants to work to start their pursuit of happiness. And I want them to succeed!

Give America A Chance

Can you feel my passion? Will you join my fight? Or will you sit on the sidelines and try to figure out how much debt you can put on your children? The government won't do it—the government shouldn't do it. I can't do it alone. But we can. Quit asking the government to save you and save yourselves. Step up and join me… Please.

November 17 Update

1. I am very proud of my sister. I am very proud of my father. I am very proud of my grandfathers and their fathers before them for serving my country… For helping to make my country great. I don't want to take what they gave me and ruin it. They gave me a safe, patriotic country. Give the same things to your kids.

2. I can't stand hearing people say they're not responsible for the current state of our nation because they didn't vote for the guy. Or worse yet, they didn't vote at all. This is still your country. There are a whole lot more presidents, congressman, senators, mayors, and other legislators in this country that I didn't vote for than those that I have voted for. The point is, however, we as a country did vote for every single one of them and we are responsible for their actions. Never forget, they work for you. They are your representatives, meaning whether you voted for them or not, their job is to represent you!

   At the beginning of the book, I mentioned that we were in debt by about 16 trillion dollars. Only a fraction of that is to China. In 2009, we owed 790 billion to them. Today, it's more than 1 trillion dollars. Scary, huh? Most of the 16 trillion is owed to ourselves. We need to pay our debt and focus on paying ourselves. Any personal banker will tell you it is important to stay out of debt and pay yourself. We can do that by buying American products. We must do that if we want our country to survive!

3. I may say this over and over, but I want to make sure I am getting this clear. I do not want the "government" to fix the problem we got ourselves into. I want the American people to fix the problem we got ourselves into. I want us to WANT us to fix our problems. Future generations NEED us to fix our problems.

4. I hear so many people telling me that it's just smart to use foreign oil first and when it runs out, we can turn and use our own. I don't believe that. That's like saying you have 100 bucks to buy a new TV, but you'd rather get a credit card and charge it. Later, when your TV breaks, you'll buy a new one with your money. I propose we buy the TV with our own cash and later on, we invent a new TV.

November 29, 2009

My apologies for waiting so long to write. I just got back from a 3,700 mile round trip vaction to Wisconsin for Thanksgiving. I took my book, intending to write, but never got the chance. I'm using this time before settling down for the night to write down some reminders about things I'd like to write about in the coming days. You can think of it as a "teaser" for what's to come... [1]

One of the first things I'd like to write about is my dream about helping the Army soldiers and the subsequent events in Chicago, IL.

Also, very important to me was our stopover at the National Cowboy Hall of Fame Museum in Oklahoma, OK. This will include the start of our Christmas ornament collection tradition.

Of course, I'll throw in a bit on Wisconsin cheese and kringle (ever heard of it?).

We really didn't do much shopping, so I can't discuss the products, but I can tell you that my wife comes from a long line of American patriots.

That said, and more to come, it feels good to be home. More than that, it feels great to be out of the truck, whew! It's back to work tomorrow. Until next time, God bless and safe travels wherever the road may lead you.

November 29 Update

1. In all honesty, I actually can't stand when I'm listening to the radio or news and they spend 30 seconds telling you about a story that they are going to tell you "after the commercial break" (a teaser). Then, when they finally get back, it only took 20 seconds to tell the entire story... Why didn't they just spend the first 30 seconds to tell the story???

Give America A Chance

November 30, 2009

A few nights ago, I had a dream that there were some Army soldiers in trouble for not obeying an unlawful order. They were given military lawyers who were told to prosecute them quickly. Now normally, I'm all about following my commander-in-chief and the officers appointed over me, but they were asked to do some ridiculous things. In my dream, I started fundraisers to get these guys some civilian lawyers who could represent them according to the law. When I woke up, I thought how odd that was... completely unlike me in real life. [1]

Allow me to interject for a second to explain a real life story that happened later that day and then I'll tie it all together.

On our trip home from Wisconsin, I got turned around in southern Chicago, IL. My wife was navigating and I asked her how to get back on the main road. We were coming up to an exit quickly and I asked her if I needed to take it. I think my exact quote was, "you have about two seconds to decide." She quickly stated "Yes, take it!" We took it and it was the right choice... We were on our way home again! I had to thank her for being decisive quickly and that in a crunch like that it was more important to make the wrong decision than not make any decision at all. We learned that in the military.

And now, I'll loop that story back to my dream. In the military, I learned quickly that when lives are in the balance, you have to make a decision. You quickly gather the best information you can get and make a plan—Then go with it. You can't leave troops on the battlefield and tell them you're thinking about it or you lose trust quickly. Our current commander-in-chief would know that if he ever unselfishly served this country. That was my AHA! moment.

My dream was about the Afghanistan war. We have troops dying over there and President Obama is "thinking" about what to do, all the while holding weekly parties at the White House and bowing to the president of China. [2]

The moral of the story is this. President Obama, our commander-in-chief, needs to decide to pull our troops out or send more troops in so we can win. Even if he makes the wrong decision, at least he would be decisive (such as a commander-in-chief should be). Please pray for our troops. They need it desperately, especially now! [3]

Give America A Chance

November 30 Update

1. It's not like I'm some sort of jerk who doesn't want to help our troops, especially when they are doing the right thing, it's just that I'm not the community organizer type of person. I don't know the first thing about organizing a fund raising event.

2. You know, he's still doing the party and golf thing... while our country falls apart. It's not that I don't respect the position. I have no doubt that being the president of the United States of America is a stressful job, but at the same time, you volunteered for the position. Heck, you fought for the position and won. I would just ask that while people are needlessly in danger, fix the situation and then have your party to celebrate, not the other way around.

3. I want to take a minute to talk about prayer... I've mentioned it several times by now. It's something that I truly believe in. A friend of my reminded me that we have an infinite God in charge of our world. The idea of infinite is nearly impossible for my mind to comprehend, but my friend said it this way; Whatever you need, even if you just need healing for a small cut on your hand, God has an infinite amount of time and an infinite amount of energy to heal your cut... and still have an infinite time and energy to spend on every other problem. One thing to remember, though, is that God's plan is not our plan. President Obama has the authority he has because God gave it to him. God has a plan for him. My goal is not to get God on my side, but to get me on God's side. That said, I will continue to pray for our troops, our president, and our country. I hope you will too.

December 2, 2009

So last night, President Obama pledged to send 30,000 more troops to Afghanistan. I will commend him on finally making a decision, but if you ask me, it's too little, too late. If you watched his announcement at West Point, you can tell the cadets were less than thrilled. And who can blame them.

First you sit on your butt for months while soldiers died. Second, you announce that you'll be sending 30,000 troops when the expert in the field asked for 40,000-60,000 additional troops. Third, you told them they'll be coming home in 18 months. Fourth, you're sending them away right before Christmas (at least some).

I could go on, but c'mon, how harsh do I need to be. You get the picture. These are not the actions of a commander-in-chief.

Let me put it this in simple perspective. Imagine you wanted to build a home for you and your family (win a war). You would seek out the best contractor (general) for the job. Then, the contractor (general) said he could do it for $100,000 (40,000-60,000 troops). When you tell the contractor (general) to do it for $80,000 (30,000 troops), what kind of house do you expect (how do you expect to win the war). The contractor (general) may do it for $80,000 (30,000 troops), but what will happen come wintertime (18 months later)? The windows will be drafty because he used substandard materials and the roof will cave in. AKA, the Taliban will re-assemble and threaten your family. Simple enough for you? [1]

On to a totally different subject. The National Cowboy and Western Heritage Museum in Oklahoma City! Boy howdy, talk about good clean family fun. We only had about an hour and a half to check it out, but we could have spent weeks. They honored past and present rodeo cowboys, American Indians, actors, including John

Wayne and Ronald Reagan, western settlers, and so much more. They even had an entire building for children to run around and play with stuff. The best part for me was the military section. They had old rifles, saddles, uniforms… they had everything. If you ever wondered how the west was really won, check it out. [2]

When we were in Wisconsin at my wife's grandma and grandpa's home, my wife took me to the attic where her great-grandfather's history came to life. Talk about a genuine patriot. I actually got to hold some of the things I was so impressed with at the museum in my own hands. Even if you didn't serve in the military, chances are some of your forefathers did. I highly recommend looking into your family history to see some of the great American patriots in your own family. Then brag about it and honor them every chance you get!

While at the museum, we picked up a Christmas ornament. Then at my wife's grandma and grandpa's house, her aunt gave us another ornament from Racine, WI (which is where we were). She said she liked to get ornaments from everywhere she visited and remember the trips come Christmas time when you're putting them up. We will continue that tradition (of course, looking for ornaments made in USA!).

We also stopped at the Cheese Castle in southern, WI. We got some fresh cheese and sausage (talk about American-made). My wife's aunt also got us kringle made in Wisconsin. If you don't know what it is, look it up online and order some (they deliver).

Well, that just about sums up our trip, leaving out the ever-so-important Thanksgiving dinner and meeting my wife's family. We had an awesome trip and will probably do it again next year.

One last mention about our trip. Most nights, we stayed at Comfort Inn's. They have hot breakfast in the morning, pools and hot tubs, and most importantly, they accept pets. One exception, though, all their soaps and shampoos were made in China. UGH! I commented this disgraceful act at every one we stayed at. Hopefully they change it for next year or we'll do a better job of finding hotels. Help me out and write them asking them to switch to American salon products… Thank you!

December 2 Update

1. I understand that the commander-in-chief has the final say and the troops should support and stand behind his decision, but it just bugs me a little bit when you call in the expert, ask his opinion, and then undermine him.
2. If there's one thing I enjoy, it's seeing the genius behind how things have changed over the years and how things used to get done. There's a great heritage museum in Alaska that goes over the Inuit history. If you ever get the chance, check it out.

Give America A Chance

December 8, 2009

Well, we're getting close to Christmas now. Besides the Christmas lights, nativity scenes, mistletoe, tree ornaments, sleigh bells, wreaths, and a feast of food, I don't think there's a whole lot else to discuss from the purchasing end... Except presents! Oh, the presents are already driving me nuts. Not only is it trying to find out what to get everybody, but then I've got to get it made in USA. I've got some thoughts and ideas which I'll discuss later, but first the other stuff. [1]

Chances are, if you get a real tree, you're getting it from somewhere in northern North America. I got a Fraser fir. I don't know its exact origin, but I can handle supporting Canada. If you get a fake tree, you're on your own. [2]

Lights? Forget about it. Everywhere I've looked, they have "other than made in USA" printed on them, usually China. Did you know that China has a "Christmas" town where all they do all year long is make Christmas stuff? Shouldn't be too surprising. I'll keep my eyes open for American-made lights, but don't get your hopes up. [3]

Nativity scenes, my favorite, are made all over. You can pretty easily find awesome hand carved, made in USA ones online. Just depends what you want... And how much you're willing to pay.

Mistletoe and wreaths are handmade by my wife. We picked up the trimmings from Lowe's and Home Depot for free and she's busy right now making them up for friends and family. By the way, mistletoe grows all over. We got ours from our backyard.

Ornaments we already talked about. It'll take some time to get a tree-full of "tourist" ornaments, but we've also got a lot of homemade stuff. Hobby Lobby had some of the do-it-yourself ornaments made in USA... Check it out.

As for the feast of food, well, that'll be easy. Most people would probably pass up a Chinese grown turkey or ham. The cranberry sauce is probably grown in Wisconsin. My wife makes a mean homemade stuffing with just bread and her special blend of spices. Add on green bean casserole and tamales and you're good to go. Yes, I said tamales. They make them right here in New Mexico and we just can't help but throw in some local flare.

But alas, we come back to the presents. I've been shopping online via madeinusaforever.com and madeinusa.org. They have some great ideas, but not every link on the site sends you to a 100% USA made site. Make sure you ask before you buy. I'm not going to give away everything that I buy, but I'll definitely pass on the more impressive things that I find. [4]

I do have one request, however, from everybody who reads this. Please do something good for someone in need over the holidays. If you have the ability to buy a needy family a feast of food, please do, but even homemade cards can bring a smile to those around you. I would especially request that you offer to bring in a couple lonely U.S. soldiers into your home if you live near a base. There's a good chance that some of these soldiers cannot afford to go home for the holidays. There's also a good chance that a military spouse has departed overseas to fight for your freedoms leaving a spouse and children home.

I suppose that's probably enough sob stories for now. Remember that you are a free American. Free to do as you choose within the law and free to celebrate anyway you want. And especially remember why you have that freedom. God bless and good night.

December 8 Update

1. It's been a few Christmas's since 2009 and although I definitely prefer American-made products, I have to admit that I haven't bought all American products every year. It's unfortunate that sometimes what you want can't be found from an American producer. That's why I'm writing this book... What I want is to easily find American-made products everywhere I go. I want to see people buying American-made products everywhere I go.
2. Now that I'm farther up north, it's easier to be sure where my tree comes from. Last year, we went to one of those "cut-your-own" Christmas tree farms. We got to have the fun of a hunt and support an American worker at the same time.
3. Still no luck on the lights.
4. Madeinusaforever.com is a great site. I recommend heading to that site and signing up for the newsletters if nothing else. If you decide to buy something, great... That means you're supporting an American supporting Americans. I think I've talked this principal before. It really works.

December 11, 2009

I was watching C-Span the other day and a caller told the reporter that he wished everybody would write down their feelings on global warming. He wanted that so that they could give it to their children so they know who to blame down the line. I'll take it one step farther and put my feelings on the subject into my book for my children and everyone else who wants to see. [1]

When I was younger, I was told that someday acid rain would wipe out this planet. I was told that in some places, the acid rain was burning through people's homes. This wasn't elementary school jabber; this was my teachers telling us this. [2]

Later, in junior high, I was told that global cooling was going to turn Texas (where I lived at the time) into the arctic and Greenland would become a hot desert.

More recently, I was told that global warming is melting the ice caps and if we don't change, we will all drown.

Now, "they" just claim "climate change".

Let me clarify something up front. I consider myself somewhat of an outdoorsman. I like clean air and clean water. When I hike and camp, I leave the wilderness as clean or cleaner than how I found it. I want my children to be able to camp in natural clean wilderness and sip water from a fresh spring just as I have.

Let me also say that I am observant about what I find when I am in the outdoors. I have found fossilized footprints of animals, dinosaurs, and humans at or near sea level. I have found seashells everywhere from the deserts of Africa to mountaintops in Alaska. And I believe there is a reason for all of it. [3]

Give America A Chance

I have also seen smog from polluting cities that have made me sick. If anybody has seen (in person, or in my case, pictures) the pollution and smog from Los Angeles back in the '70's and '80's, you know it was sickening. [4]

I don't ever want to see that in my country. I'd prefer not to have it on my planet, but I can't control everybody. I can vote, though!

I believe that we, as the human race, do not have much control over the climate of the earth. I don't think that if everybody painted their rooftops white, it would cool the earth any more than asking everybody to kick on their heaters in the winter and keep their doors open will keep an entire city at 75 degrees. Plainly put, I don't believe in the "media" term of global warming, cooling, or climate change.

If the magnetic poles of the earth are shifting, and they are, there's not a whole lot we can do about it. I've seen glaciers in Alaska receded on one side miles and miles in just 40 or 50 years (or at least that's what the signs say). I've also seen the other side of the glaciers freezing and wiping out forests. I believe they shift, move, and slide wherever they want to. [5]

Basically, I don't put a lot of stock in "modern" science. My great aunt used to live on a lake and she would record the date the lake froze over every year. Sometimes it would happen later. And sometimes it would freeze over sooner. Climate change, to me, is something that happens four times per year and we call it seasons. [6]

Now all that said, I'd like to see alternative energy solutions as well. Not because I think we're running out of coal and oil (I think there's plenty to go around), but because I really like innovations. I would love to see solar panels get so common and so affordable; I can discreetly put them on my roof and power my whole house. I would love to see something better come along some day. I don't know what it is, but maybe you do. Awesome, lets run with all the new ideas and see who crosses the finish line. [7]

Until then, don't look down on me for driving a 15MPG truck. There was more I wanted to touch on today including some things I ordered for Christmas, but that will have to wait now. I didn't tell you all of this to change your mind. I did it because some caller on some TV show asked everybody to do it. Different opinions have different solutions. That's what makes this country so great. One guy believes oil is ruining the world, so he or she finds ideas to save it. Another guy depends on oil to get supplies to the first guy so he can make it happen. It's a great big world with great big ideas and a great big future. I won't knock down either guy and neither should anybody else as long as no one gets hurt. Just don't get in my way as I am in my God given, constitution protected, pursuit of happiness. [8]

December 11 Update

1. It's funny to me... There's quite a bit of people who wrote down their feelings on the matter years ago. We laugh at them now. There were reports from the 60's and 70's that said every man, woman, and child would have to wear a gas mask by the year 2000.
2. Now apparently there have been cases where the rainfall was so polluted that it made people sick. And living here in California, even in the mountains, the smog can get so bad I can't see the mountain I live on from the city. But this doesn't mean there's a global phenomenon. Keep reading... I explain more.
3. Have you ever thought about why there are seashells at the tops of mountains? I used to find them a mile up in the mountains of New Mexico all the time. Think about it.
4. Those pictures were literally disgusting. It's ingrained into my mind forever. I hope we never go back to that level of pollution. It makes the people in the city sick. It even has the potential to kill people. But even that horrible, terrible, no good, very bad smog wasn't permanently changing the climate only a few miles away.
5. I recently read that the South Pole ice caps are larger now than they have been in recorded history. Does that mean that the sea level went down a few feet? I'm just asking.
6. Modern science does a lot of great things. We've essentially wiped out some of the diseases that used to kill entire cities. We've invented and improved a lot of things. I guess that was an overstatement on my part. With that, though, we've also blown a lot of hot air.
7. I'm completely serious about this. If you have an idea for a cheap energy solution, I want to hear it. Heck, I probably want a part of it. But don't tell me that you're going to give me a type of fuel for my truck that will destroy the inner workings of my combustion engine, cost more money, and reduce my fuel efficiency. Ethanol... Shouldn't we be eating that corn and wiping out global hunger by using gasoline and diesel fuel to ship the rest of the corn to the corners of the earth?
8. Well, like I said in the title of the book... The rants and raves of a true American patriot. You've been getting a bit more of the rants lately. Don't worry... I'll get back to the raves soon.

Give America A Chance

December 15, 2009

I've got a couple made in USA items to broadcast, along with a funny story and a ranting about naked people and gang violence. Since I don't want to get carried away with nonsense, let me tell you about two made in USA products I got for Christmas gifts.

The first is a knife set from Rada Cutlery. This is a gift, so obviously I haven't used them. They appear to be quality, the online ratings were pretty high, and best of all, they came with a certificate stating they were made in the USA.

The other is a dollhouse for my daughter. Last week, my wife went to Hobby Lobby to look for an American-made dollhouse. They had a few and she got one from Greenleaf. Now, it's not a cheapo plastic thing you would probably find elsewhere. This looks like a real nice wooden dollhouse…kit. That's where the affordable comes into play. It's a kit, so I'll build it and my wife will paint it. Two great things about it… very affordable and made in the USA! [1]

So my folks were in town again last weekend. My parents know about my attempt at a book and the reason I'm writing it. They're supportive, but my dad is a bit "unsure" of this mission of mine. He's right when he tells me there is so much wrong with this world, "you need to pick and choose your battles." Well, I've picked and chosen this battle, along with many others (hence the rants and raves). We were fixin' to go to a hardware store and I told him I wanted some eyebolts to put up Christmas lights. He casually mentioned, well, "you won't find any made in the USA," to which I responded, "then I won't get any, but I bet I'll find some." Luckily I found National brand eye bolts. Yup, made in USA! By the way, we were at ACE Hardware. [2]

Now on to naked people. Sounds a bit silly, right? What if I told you a naked man was walking outside your children's school just as school let out... your elementary school! Not so funny anymore, is it?

In Ashland, Oregon, it is legal to roam around town naked. So much that unless you're in a public park or building, you can go 100% nude. That's just what one pervert did. He was making laps around the high school, middle school, and then finally the elementary school when school let out for the day.

Now you say, "call the cops!" That's exactly what happened. Children were crying and parents got upset. The police came to protect the man from the angry parents... WHAT!?!?? Allow me a second to jump on my high horse and exclaim, "WHAT THE HECK HAPPENED TO OUR SOCIETAL MORALS?" This guy should have been declared a pervert, arrested, and clothed. If you want to be nude, fine. Do it at home or in one of those "clothing optional" resorts, but don't subject innocent children to your perverted fantasies. [3]

Oh, and last, but not least... Gang violence. Or should I say cowardly wars over your "turf?" Last Sunday evening, my mother, father, wife, daughter, and I stopped at a local gas station/convenience store. None of us were feeling too great so my wife and I went in to get ice cream and brandy (to make "hot toddies). We were just leaving when we heard three gunshots and saw people literally diving into the store. Please keep in mind, my innocent 7 year old daughter is sitting in the car in the parking lot with her grandparents.

Fear? You bet! Panic? Just a little. I got my wife safe and while people are still flooding into the store, I ran out to check on my family. Luckily we were all safe, but seriously, a drive-by in a nice neighborhood on a Sunday? What is this? I call it cowards. That's right. If you're in a gang that promotes violence when there are innocent bystanders, you are a coward. You are not what makes this country great. You are not a hero. You are a coward. So now, one more fight. Let's lock up these cowards. Be safe! [4]

December 15 Update

1. I think I mention this later on, but it took a long time to put this together... Especially since we had to do it after my daughter had gone to sleep. It was fun, though.
2. I mention ACE Hardware quite a few times in this book... I really like those stores. The one near my house has worked with me on pricing a few times. Not because the product was cheaper somewhere else, they weren't, but simply because I didn't want to pay what they were asking so I asked for a deal. Can't beat that.
3. This is the part that really shocked me... The police protected the naked man. Granted, he wasn't breaking the laws of the town, but the least they could have done was escort him away. Now... People of Ashland, OR... If you don't like it, change your laws by voting as a community.
4. Maybe I should be just glad the police didn't show up and protect the shooter.

December 17, 2009

I'm pretty excited. Today I received my first order from MadeinUSAforever.com. I'm not going to go over every item I ordered, but I will say that I am extremely happy with everything I received and how I received it. Everything was well packaged and there was even a hand written "thank you" note from Todd Lipscomb, the founder and president. He included some business cards which I will certainly pass out along with some pens for advertising. The pens are star spangled red, white, and blue and have "Doing Something Real for our Economy" written on them. [1]

That's really all I had for today, but I'd like to also pass some stuff I've been waiting to pass on. About 6 months ago, I went to Wal-Mart with my daughter to get new razors. I usually get the Gillette Mach 3, but I was comparing some of the other brands when my daughter chimed in, "These are made in the USA." Sure enough, there were some disposable razors whose blades are made in the USA. I picked up a package of 10 for a fraction of the price of 5 Gillette refills.

I've been using them now for 6 months and still haven't used them all up. I waited to mention them because I don't want to advertise "junk." But I will say that Personna brand triple blade "Speed 3" are every bit as good as the stuff I used to use before. I picked up a package of men's (green) and women's (pink). My wife agrees that they're as good as the others. [2]

One last note of thought. Farmers Markets. We have a farmers market in town every Wednesday and Saturday. Most of the products are handmade locally. The best part is, they have quality stuff at great prices. I encourage you to check the happenings in your community. The only thing better than keeping your money in your country is keeping it in your community.

December 17 Update

1. I have ordered from MadeinUSAforever a few times over the years. If nothing else, I highly recommend checking out the site and recommending it to your friends and family. It's a great way to spread the word about buying American-made products easily.
2. After 3 years, still great products. There are some other "cheaper" brands out there that are made in USA as well. I will buy an item that has the "Made in USA" stamp over another that doesn't any day.

December 26, 2009

Well, we made it through Christmas and enjoyed every second of it… at least most of it. There were a couple things that I noticed in the immediate pre-Christmas shopping days.

I went to Wal-Mart to look for small trinkets and chocolates. I noticed something that really made me think. As I was checking out a particular item, I first looked at the back of the package to see where it was made and noticed "Made in PRC." Perhaps this has been going on for a while, but I've never noticed it before. I think most intelligent people can easily identify that as the People's Republic of China, but I'm sure some people, in an effort to avoid Chinese products have been duped by the "PRC." [1]

Later, when I was checking out, I started a conversation with the gentleman in front of me. We were discussing some massive 4' tall stuffed animals and how cheap they were. I checked the tag and commented, "Yea, but do you really want to throw all that Chinese stuffing in with your kids?" (By the way, I was not criticizing something he purchased; rather the stuffed animals were in the center aisle.) He replied back by saying there's no way around it, holding up his can of Minwax stain. I quickly re-assured him that Minwax is made in USA and that by going to MadeinUSAforever.com, he could also get USA made stuffed animals.

What amazes me is two things. First, China's attempt to "hide" the origin of the products either via made in PRC, Hong Kong, China, or whatever clever name they come up with next. And secondly, Americans feeling as though they are trapped and forced to buy Chinese products.

We are all free Americans, right? There's no reason to feel trapped. There are plenty of quality made items at very affordable prices made right here. You are free to buy whatever you like, Chinese or otherwise. I'm not trying to take that right away, but I do want to encourage all patriots of America to help out their country.

Let me point out one more quick example/challenge for you. Run down to your local Wal-Mart and go to the aisle with flashlights. You'll no doubt find flashlights ranging from 5 bucks to 50 bucks and higher. Grab a Maglight and a comparable competitor's item in the same price range. The Maglight you know is quality. Aircraft aluminum, spare bulb in the bottom, easy to find batteries for, sturdy, and best of all, made in the USA. Now check out the competitors. Plastic? No spare bulb? Odd battery size? Does it feel sturdy? And where is it made? Exactly. Now check out toothbrushes… coffee pots… hand tools… heck, even Craftsman used to be made in the USA and came with lifetime warranties. Now most are made in China with "limited" warranties. [2]

It's sad to see so many companies outsourcing to China and other countries, but you don't have to outsource what you buy. Just takes a bit more time to shop around.

I've been on a strong "made in USA" kick for over a year now and writing about it for nearly 5 months. Hang in there and we'll get this country back up and running again. Don't give up on me now. Don't fall for the naming tricks and don't feel trapped. We can do this!

December 26 Update

1. In the past few years, I've been avoiding Wal-Mart like the plague. I discuss it often, because in my previous location, it was the best place to go to get what you need. Forced by necessity in my new place, I've found it isn't the best and probably wasn't the best back then either. That said, I'm finding lots of new ways that the PRC is changing the way it labels its products. Most recently, I've found labels indicating the actual city the products are coming from. I think it's a method of personifying the products.
2. Hopefully, you notice that as more outsourcing is done, the warranties are lower as well. The warranties are lower because the quality is lower. Despite the problems with this country, finding quality workers to make quality products isn't one of them.

Give America A Chance

January 3, 2010

I did not make a New Year's resolution. If you did, I hope it was to support the greatest nation on Earth a little bit more. I did, however, spend a lot of money for new appliances in my home. My family and I shopped everywhere for a new stove, refrigerator, dishwasher, and over the stove microwave. I don't want to say the equipment we had was old, but I do believe Thomas Jefferson may have used my stove at one time.

Actually, it's a great Tappan gas stove with a double oven. It was made in the USA and has worked flawlessly for us. We just needed an upgrade. (1)

We ended up buying from Lowe's. We had a 10% off coupon, but I could have earned the 10% off with my military discharge paperwork. (2)

We went with Whirlpool. The range is made in USA. The dishwasher and refrigerator are supposed to also be made in the USA, we'll see upon delivery. Unfortunately, the microwave is made in the "People's Republic of China." I didn't have a choice in that category. (3)

Everything should be delivered in the next 4 weeks. If you want an honest assessment of Whirlpool appliances, stay tuned... I'll give you updates from my first assessment to every detail that we like, don't like, and problems we hopefully won't have.

The saleslady at Lowe's actually asked why we want made in America. I simply stated that this is my country and I'd like to keep America working. I think she was a little shocked at that.

On a separate note, my sister-in-law commented on how much she and her 2 young boys liked the toys we got for them for Christmas. We got them some solid wood, quality trucks, and a helicopter from MadeinUSAforever.com. We also got them a kitchen knife set from there.

And on another separate note, remember the doll house we got for our daughter? The kit? It was very affordable and made in the USA, but it was a time consuming project. If you pick one up in the future, leave ample time for assembly. We finished it on Christmas Eve. It turned out great and I love watching my daughter play with it, but it wasn't fun to put together. Would I do it again, you bet! Just heed my caution... You can't just throw it together in a couple hours and call it quits. But since everything, including the instructions, were made here, it was very easy to follow along. Doing it in secret, late at night, was the tricky part. [4]

Until next time, stay patriotic, buy American, and do you part for your country. God bless!

January 3 Update

1. We ended up selling that stove locally to a guy who needed a good stove. I'd be willing to bet that stove is still working wonderfully somewhere.
2. Apparently, Lowe's went away with the 10% program unless you're active duty. I don't know if that's true.
3. The reason I said the dishwasher and refrigerator are supposed to be made in USA rather than are made in USA is because even though the floor models were made in USA, it's no guarantee every individual product actually is.
4. Funny story about the dollhouse… The dollhouse was from Santa. As my wife and I were assembling the dollhouse, my family was taking pictures. On Christmas day, my daughter asked to see my visiting family's camera. She was looking through the photos, and saw the pictures of my wife and me assembling it. Fortunately, she figured out that Santa bought the dollhouse and we just assembled it for her.

January 7, 2009

I got my first delivery of Whirlpool products yesterday. But first, I need to vent.

If you recall, about a month ago, I vented about Obama taking so long to take the advice from his generals regarding the war in Afghanistan. I was upset because the general he chose to advise him told Obama what he needed to win the war. After several months of intense deliberation which included vacations, parties, concerts, golf games, etc... Obama chose his own route.

Now, on Christmas day, 2009, a cowardly terrorist planted explosives in his underwear and tried to blow up a passenger jet over the United States. Yes, I said cowardly and yes I said terrorist... get over it. [1]

A few days after the failed attack, Obama came out and threw his intelligence team under a steam roller and said it was an intelligence failure.

The buck stops... somewhere over there, right? [2]

Do you see the point I'm making? Obama's intelligence teams can advise him all they want, but he's proven over and over that he will do whatever he wants as long as it doesn't interrupt his Hawaiian vacation, while innocent civilians are at risk, putting their safety in line! ARGH! Can you feel my anger yet? Will this president ever take responsibility? Perhaps we can blame this on Bush as well. [3]

Anyway, I got my Whirlpool refrigerator and microwave delivered yesterday. The fridge states "Assembled in the USA" as I had hoped and the microwave says made in PRC as I expected. Just as reminder, PRC stands for People's Republic of China. The fridge is Awesome! We emptied the old one and filled the new one. Our old one, buy the way, was full. The new one is only half full now... It's that big. We got the Whirlpool Gold with the Freezer door beneath. It's 22 cubic feet and claims to take less energy in a year than a 60 watt light bulb. Cool, huh? My only complaint so far is the icemaker is slower than the old one. It's been operating for 24 hours now and the ice bucket isn't full yet. Other than that, we love it. [4]

I have to wait for my stove to arrive before hooking up the microwave. Again though, it's huge. It's the over-the-stove model with a vent. We at first, questioned if it will fit, but after measuring, it's the same width as the vent attached to my current stove, so it should be just fine. I'll let you know more when we get it working.

On a separate note, I went back up to Lowe's to get firewood and a chimney sweep. We're expecting a cold front. The chimney sweeps they had there were all made in China, so I'll probably just hire a local contractor rather than buy Chinese products. But on a good note, I found an electric heater made in USA. King brand electric baseboard heaters. If you need extra heat, don't get the other stuff, go for the King!

Now, stay warm, support your country, and go do good things!

January 7 Update

1. Did it bother anybody else that nobody wanted to call the guy who did this a terrorist for a long time?
2. So hold on a second… You want the advice of the experts, but you sit on that advice for months. Then, when you finally make a decision, it's your decision, not the expert advice you wanted.
3. After all, everything is Bush's fault, right? Even after being re-elected (something I don't understand) there are still things being blamed on the previous administration. I am so glad the previous administration didn't blame things on his previous administration and I hope the next administration doesn't take the easy way out either.
4. Years later and I still have that refrigerator… When we left New Mexico, this fridge came with us. Unfortunately, it's sitting unused in the garage right now since it's about 1-inch too tall for the house we are renting. We finally got the idea of selling it, but when I posted it on Craigslist.com, I jacked the price knowing it wouldn't sell for the amount I was asking. I figured if it wouldn't sell for that price, I didn't want to sell it. I still use it every so often, but most of the time, it just sits.

January 10, 2010

Up until this very point, I have been writing with an American-made Pilot G-2 pen. However, right now, I am writing with a Chinese knock-off of a Picasso fountain pen. Before you criticize, allow me to explain. A good friend returned from China yesterday. Before he left, I asked him to get me something made in the USA.

Unfortunately, he was unable to find anything so he got me a quite nice fountain pen. He got his daughter a "Coach" purse. I won't go into a detail on his trip, but two things that he mentioned the most was the pollution and mistreatment of women. Other than that, he had a great trip and was treated like a king. [1]

Now, allow me to brag on an American-made product. I've mentioned that we got an American Whirlpool refrigerator. The old one had water and ice in the door. Nice, but it takes up valuable space in the freezer. The bad part is that we were left without filtered water. [2]

Our solution? An under-the-sink water filter. There were a few different brands, all made in China. We've all heard, and I just mentioned the pollution in China. I do not want that filtering my water. We got a 3M Filtrete water filtration system… Made in USA with USA and imported materials. Heck, at least some of it was made right here at home. We've had it for a few weeks now and really enjoy it. The water tastes great, but best of all, there is no change to my sink setup. It comes straight out of the cold water tap. Plus, it was a cinch to install.

In other news, Brunswick has decided to sell out and move their bowling ball plant to Mexico putting many Americans out of work. They claim they can't afford union labor. There are a lot of "right to work" states that would have loved to accept them, but I guess the American standard has just lowered. I, for one, don't plan on buying anything other than an American-made bowling ball. [3]

Until then thank you for being a patriot and continue to buy American products as much as possible. I certainly don't regret it and I know you won't either.

January 10 Update

1. I was really hoping he would be able to find something. I don't think he had the time to do a bunch of in-depth shopping so maybe there is something there, but I don't know. If anybody reading this has ever been to China, let me know what they sell there that is made in USA. I'd be really curious.
2. It's a big deal for us to have lots of freezer space. First of all, the amount of ice cream that my family eats is a bit ridiculous and I don't ever plan on taking that away. Secondly, I like to buy in bulk, so buying 10lbs of ground beef, 10 steaks, and 30 chicken breasts and all the other frozen goodies and there's not a whole lot of room left.
3. Their website still says all their bowling balls are made in Mexico. I honestly don't get it. People from Mexico are moving to the USA for jobs while some companies are moving their jobs to Mexico. The immigration issue is separate issue, but the jobs thing is what really gets me. I really, really want to get our Americans working. Unions or non-unions. Get our Americans working! I hear about unions shutting down American companies all the time and it really "ticks" me off. If you're a union employee and you're trying to shut down an American company because they don't want to unionize, shame on you! You are NOT a patriot. Getting a better job with better pay is one thing… you're not going to get that by chasing the job you wanted to another country.

January 13, 2010

I don't have a whole lot to speak of today. I'll just quickly tell you about a couple products.

The first, Channel Lock pliers. I needed a new set of pliers so I shot to Home Depot to see what they had. In a bright blue package with an American flag and "Made in the USA" right on the front were Channel Lock pliers. And you know what; they were cheaper than the Chinese competitors. But I thought Americans couldn't compete with Chinese pricing? There's more. [1]

Today, my wife went to Hobby Lobby to find a wood burning kit for a project she's working on. She found one made in Indonesia, but she wasn't impressed with it (and it wasn't American-made), so she passed on it.

Later, she went to a local store called the Frame and Art shop here in Las Cruces. She found a wood burning kit of better quality, more options, Made in USA, and only a few dollars more. But it continues... [2]

Yesterday, I picked up a small day planner at Office Max. I got a "Day Minder" from MWV Consumer and Office Products for quite a bit cheaper than the similar products that did not say where they were made. [3]

On a separate note, I was listening to the Great One yesterday on the radio... Now since I told you I would tell the name the next time I mentioned him, his name is Mark Levin. He recently wrote a book titled "Liberty and Tyranny: A Conservative Manifesto." He was discussing a little bit on why he wrote it and mentioned that most people thought we were in hopeless times. Some had rolled over and given up. Similarly, that is why I started this book. Most people I talk to say it's pointless to buy American products. "Everything is made in China now days." Bull Honky Tonk! I say, the best products are made right here by your friends and neighbors. There's no reason to give in! There's no reason to give up! If we give up, we've lost... and I am not a loser. Americans are not losers and America is not a losing nation. Hard times or not, America is a great nation and we can make it better. [4]

Now, do something right for your country... DO something right for Americans and do something right for the American economy. Roll over and give up? Yea, right!

January 13 Update

1. Ask any man and they will tell you that there is something special about a good tool. Get them tools made in the USA and they won't complain. In fact, I'd venture to say that most men will recognize the quality immediately.
2. My wife has always been a bit frugal, but now that she's looking for the "Made in USA" label, frugal is actually quite a bit easier.
3. Don't let anybody tell you that there's nothing made in the USA anymore. It's not true. Don't let them tell you that all American-made products are more expensive. That's not true either. Don't take my word for it… Look for yourself.
4. I do believe that some Americans have rolled over and given up. Not me.
You may be wondering why Mark Levin is called "the Great One." Well, from my understanding, it has to do with a nickname Sean Hannity gave him. The nickname stuck and, well, that's the story. If you listen to Mr. Levin, you'll soon realize that this man is passionate about what he discusses and he doesn't mince words in the slightest bit.

Give America A Chance

January 17, 2010

My daughter is with her grandparents today, so my wife and I decided to go see Avatar in 3D at the theater. We also did some shopping after church this morning. So I got good and bad today. Please keep in mind that the bad to come is only my opinion, but for that matter, so is the good. Anyway, on with it.

I'll start with the good. After church, my wife, daughter, and I headed down to the New Balance outlet store near El Paso, TX. I've written on them in the past. But now, I desperately needed shoes. My 2 pair of tennis shoes both had holes in the sides and no more traction on the soles. My wife and I agreed (equally) to join a team to do a Bataan Memorial March, a 26-mile hike with over a 1,000-foot elevation change. If you don't know the history of the Bataan Death March, do some research, a lot of brave men died. [1]

Back to the shoes. We ended getting four pairs of shoes, made in the USA, for under $110! I got 2 pairs, the 479 and 609. My wife got a pair of 609 and my daughter got a pair of 571. I also got a 20% military discount... Thank you! New Balance produces 25% of their shoes (7,000,000) in the US. To qualify the "Made in USA" label, the domestic value has to be at least 70% according to the label and the Federal Trade Commission. I got that information from one of the shoe labels by the way. They also claim to be the only athletic footwear manufacturer in the USA. Please help support them by buying their USA made shoes. [2]

Just as a side note, when I joined the Air Force back in 1995, they provided us with New Balance shoes for our physical conditioning. I don't recall if they were made in the USA or not.

We also got our Whirlpool stove and dishwasher delivered over the weekend. I had to do some work to get the stove and microwave installed which included re-piping my propane lines and some electrical work. FYI, I got Scotch vinyl electrical tape made in USA with the American flag and quote printed proudly on the front. I also got twisting wire connectors from Ideal Industries, Inc. for much cheaper than the competitor's brands. They also have the American flag and "Made in USA" clearly printed on the front. And finally, I got a Brass Craft gas installation kit. They've got "manufactured in U.S.A. on the bottom of the box.

OK, onto my movie review. The graphics were great, the 3D experience was decent, the action was fun, but the storyline stunk! Not because of the action, but because of the bad guys. After several mentions of the Marines, the primary actor mentions quietly that they were more along the lines of hired mercenaries in it for the money. Later in the movie, you get the impression that they, "the Marines," were hired by some corporation to deal with the local population. My wording, not the movie's. By the end of the movie, you have the local population as well as some Americans turning against the US soldiers and killing them. That's the part I really didn't like. [3]

Remember the movie Hellboy or Indiana Jones? They both fought against the Nazi's... Everybody hates the Nazi's. Why couldn't James Cameron go that route? Make the enemy a common enemy, not our own people. I've fought with our military and yes, we're gung-ho about protecting this nation against all enemies foreign and domestic. And yes, sometimes some people go overboard, but that's the kind of action that is dealt with swiftly within the military. Our soldiers are not baby-killers and murderers. If you liked the movie, great, but don't expect to walk out feeling overwhelmingly proud of our country.

Please keep in mind that our country is awesome and a lot of brave heroes have died to keep it that way. Don't let Hollywood affect your pride.

January 17 Update

1. Just to mention in here one more thing... Church was good too. I should have said that from the get-go. We were going to Mesilla Park Community Church in Las Cruces with Pastor Diaz. It's a great church that is continually working on ways to make it easy for people in the city to attend church. Check it out sometime.
2. I just threw out one of the pairs of shoes. After almost four years of wear, they deserved nothing but the dumpster. I am very hard on shoes. These were some of the best pairs of shoes I have ever owned.
3. I've pretty much given up on expecting Hollywood to make a pro-America movie. Captain America was pretty good, but that was because of one superhero... The "generals" wanted to keep him as an icon rather than a war hero. If you were to ask a real military commander if they'd rather have a superhero act as an icon or a soldier, they'll probably tell you they already have superhero's working for them.

January 24, 2010

Since I don't have a great deal of topics tonight, I'd like to tell you a little about a family trip we took this weekend and then hop on my soapbox for a few seconds. Also, earlier today, we got the Whirlpool Gold dishwasher finally installed. The first load is washing now, so I'll talk about my opinions of that at a later date. [1]

My wife, daughter, and I took a quick trip to Mesa, Arizona this weekend to visit family. My folks and grandmother were vacationing there. We went to this great pizza joint called the Organ Stop Pizza. The pizza was reasonably priced and delicious, but it's not the pizza that highlighted the evening... It was the entertainment!

They had a "Mighty Wurlitzer" organ, something I didn't even know existed. This is not your average church organ. This thing controls nearly 6,000 pipes, 17 percussion instruments, and a boatload of traps and other sound effects, not to mention trumpets, clarinets, tubas, flutes, and all sorts of other horns. It even controlled an accordion and stringed instruments. This particular Wurlitzer is the largest in the world.

On the particular night we were there, the awesome Charlie Balogh was playing... Awesome is an understatement. When he played a military tribute which included the anthems of the U.S. Marine Corps, Navy, Army, Coast Guard, and Air Force, our entire family and many others jumped to our feet for a standing ovation.

If you're ever in the area, and this is reason enough to go, I'll give you address: 1149 East Southern Avenue, Mesa, AZ 85204.

Now, onto my soapbox... We have been discussing getting another dog. We have a black Labrador retriever who is 11 years old and in great shape. She's AKC registered. I bought Audi when she was only 2 months old and she's been at my side pretty much ever since. I like Labradors because they're large enough for protection, active enough for hunting, and extremely loyal.

On the way home, we decided to look at another AKC registered puppy. When I bought Audi, I checked and double checked pedigree's and made sure the mother and father were there so I could see what I could expect. Unfortunately, the puppy we went to look at only had the father on site. Although the puppy seemed healthy and active, we decided against her because the mother was not on site. I am a firm believer that the only reason to breed pets is to improve the breed. [2]

I got Audi spayed because her great-grandmother was also her great-great grandmother. Too much inbreeding to continue the lineage—a mistake. Audi's a great example of the Labrador breed. [3]

But if you have pets, please get them spayed or neutered. Many places have clinics for very cheap or even free. There are so many pets that are in pounds and kennels because people don't want them. Getting your pet spayed or neutered prevents the unwanted pets. If you have a pet from a good bloodline and is in excellent health, please don't breed it with anything that comes along. Check the pedigree and again, only breed if it would improve the breed.

I've been to a few other countries where dogs run rampant. It's horrible for me to see flea-ridden, possibly even rabid, dogs rummaging through trash cans. I believe that we, Americans, should hold ourselves to a higher standard because of everything we stand and fight for.

Ok, off my soapbox. Have a great night and sleep in peace.

January 24 Update

1. You've read enough by now to know that my soapboxes usually last more than a second… I'm going to ask you to keep something in mind as I hop on my soapboxes… I'm definitely not trying to say that I'm better than anybody who may be reading this. As a matter of fact, I can freely admit that I have millions of faults. My purpose is to simply play out my opinions… It is your right to take it or leave it as your see fit. We are in a free country. I should never have to tell anybody that it is your right to take my opinions (or leave them), but in today's environment, some people's opinions seem to be a whole lot more than just that (health care anybody?).

2. As a quick aside, there is nothing wrong with buying a pet from a local shelter or buying a dog without knowing their pedigree. This is a personal preference of mine, but I have known many "mutts" and strays that have made totally awesome pets. There are people, some of my friends included, who prefer mutts to purebreds, and will swear by abilities and loyalties. I cannot argue with them, they are just as right as anybody else.

3. When I say, "a mistake," what I am referring to is my choice to get Audi spayed. She was, by far, the best dog I have ever had or known. She was my loyal companion for years. She protected me from wolves in Alaska, she fetched food while we were in the wilderness, she warned me of danger, and best of all, she was a friend.

   A few months ago, Audi stopped eating. She gave me "the look" that told me she was ready to die. I was faced with a very difficult decision--I made the appointment at a vet and, the next day, while my wife drove to the vet, I carried Audi in my lap giving her the love she deserved. When we arrived, my entire family went in and held her. The vet told us exactly what to expect and gave her the injection that would end her life.

   While my entire family cried, myself included, Audi took her last breath with her head in my arms.

   Although it was the right thing to do, and after as many years with her, I knew it was what she wanted, it was still extremely hard to accept her passing. It is now, still, hard to accept her passing.

   In her memory, I am planning to write a children's book that will commemorate her life, with my wife, the best and only artist in the world who can capture her personality, illustrating.

   With all that said, I urge you to care for your pets. It is the right thing to do. It is the moral thing to do. It is so important, that even King Solomon urged his people to care for their animals in Proverbs 12:10.

February 1, 2010

I realize that there are some large gaps between writing some days. But like I've said before, I don't buy stuff every day. In fact, the only things I've bought over the past week were groceries and hay for the horses. Obviously, today's writing is not about more American-made products. I did, however, rent a Bobcat over the weekend to do some yard work. It certainly turns a week's work of heavy raking, chopping, digging, and stacking a much easier weekend task.

I would like to go over some of the recent news. Osama Bin Laden apparently came out with another video tape. He claimed that America is responsible for global warming. If I remember correctly, we're one of the leading nations pursuing cleaner technology. Anyway, when our enemies are calling on a boycott of American goods, I say buy more. [1]

Unfortunately, Glenn Beck mentioned that we, as Americans, cost too much to make anything here in America. I have to call you out on that one Mr. Beck. My experiences have led me to believe something different. Of course, Mr. Beck was referring to the unions and red-tape regulations. He's right on target with that. I certainly hope to see more states turn to "right-to-work" states and I'd love to see government butt out of free enterprise and corporations. [2]

I didn't watch the State of the Union address by President Obama. He's too eloquent a speaker and his words mean nothing. Maybe if he starts honoring his promises, I'll watch more of him. Though I did watch his Q&A with the House Republicans. [3]

It was interesting to see him turn all the questions back on the people who asked questions without actually answering the questions. I'd really like to see him implement a "buck stops here" mentality versus blaming everybody else. [4]

I suppose we'll just have to wait and see if he takes responsibility for anything, including his own words and ideas, in the future. Until then, hang on for the ride. This is still the best nation on earth. And we, as Americans, ultimately hold the power for change. Let's just make sure we do it correctly. [5]

Give America A Chance

February 1 Update

1. In more detail, Bin Laden called for the wheels of the American economy to stop. I can't say it any more clearly... whatever out enemies want us do to, we should probably do the opposite. Bin Laden is gone now, but the idea remains. There are many out there who want us to stop making American goods. There are many nations that won't buy American-made goods (even though the people in those nations want and need it). When I ask you to buy American-made products, I'm not doing so because I want other countries to fail... My basic principle is simple. I want America to succeed. We can only do that by keeping our economy strong. We can only keep our economy strong by putting Americans to work. We can only put Americans to work it they have a job to go to. Buy American products!

2. Since I'm fairly sure that I've made my stance fairly clear on how I feel about unions that get in the way of an American business (I'm not criticizing the unions themselves, or what they originally stood for, but I do criticize when they get greedy), I'm don't want to go into it too much more, but it'll probably come up again. Just a warning.

3. I have spent hours listening to our President. I respect the position of the President of the United States despite who is in office, so I listen. But I am honestly getting sick of hearing President Obama say things that I fully agree with, but he never follows through. I'm also getting sick of the blaming and double-talk.

4. Why can't politicians ever answer a yes or no question? What are they hiding?

5. Well, I've waited and waited... I don't believe he's taken responsibility to a darn thing. I think he's finally over blaming President Bush, but now it's Congress that gets the blame. Or anybody else who might be handy.

February 3, 2010

There's a lot of talk in the news about giving terrorists Miranda Rights. This is something that's been bugging me lately so I feel the need to express my thoughts on the issue. ⁽¹⁾

I think there should be a distinct difference between law enforcement within America's borders and military enforcement outside our borders. If a terrorist or suspected terrorist is captured within our borders by law enforcement personnel, perhaps they should be entitled to a lawyer and our judicial system. ⁽²⁾

My issues is on the other side, or the "outside" aspect. Our military fights to keep the battle away from our homes and family. If they are captured, chances are, they were doing something wrong. Obviously it needs to be proven, but not through our American civilian judicial system.

Our military heroes fight to stop attacks, not to wait for the attack so they have enough information to prosecute them. Think about it. If our forces have intelligence that an attack is going to take place, they need the freedom to stop the attack and save lives. Some of the information they receive may come from an informant that they need to keep secret. The last thing we want to do is put that informant on the judicial bench for the world to see. That would put the informant's life in danger and stop future information. ⁽³⁾

That's my two cents. And for all the military heroes putting their life on the line, thank you… You've got my full support.

February 3 Update

1. The title says, "rants and raves," there's been a lot more of the rants lately... I will get back to our products later, but sometimes, I've just got to vent. Not only that, but this is true history. As I go back and read some of what I wrote about, I forgot that I wrote it. Even more, I forgot about the entire situation. It's amazing how history repeats itself again and again. Wait until you get to February 15, 2010... There's history repeating itself more and more.
2. I believe this because there's not always a way for a police officer to identify the nationality or intent of a potential terrorist. If a police officer finds out what's going on using their normal police channels, chances are there's enough information to convict anyway. Military, on the other hand...
3. The military has "special" methods of gathering information (and I'm not advocating phone tapping on Americans, don't get me wrong). Those special methods need to be protected. Whether it be military intelligence or a foreigner who crossed sides, those methods need to remain classified. We can't give all the information to a lawyer and let them run free with that information. Generally, when you have a secret, you don't go around blabbing it to the entire world. Military secrets should be no different, especially when it comes to people's lives.

The Rants and Raves of an American Patriot

February 11, 2010

I feel quite overdue for writing, especially about my Whirlpool appliances. But first, a couple things. And no, I don't want to discuss the Iranian Revolution Anniversary. That is not something I believe is appropriate to celebrate or worthy of discussion. Way more important is Valentine's Day is coming up.

Men, what have you gotten your wives (or girlfriends)? I haven't been married that long and as a man, I know this is a corny holiday. But our women, whether or not they think it's corny, expect some thought and consideration on our part. Even kids play roles in this game. [1]

Yesterday, my daughter and I went up to Target to look for Valentine's Day cards for her classmates. It sounds odd to me that my 7-year old daughter was giving out cards with special sayings and hearts, but I suppose it's harmless enough. Here's what gets me though, do you remember those little candy hearts with witty sayings on them? I wanted to get them for my daughter and her class, but they were made in China. They can hardly make toys without having safety recalls and now they're making things for our kids to eat… I think not. We bought a 300-count bag of Dum-Dum's for less than 7 bucks, and they were made in the USA… Even had Old Glory printed on the bag. [2]

Now on to the Whirlpool kitchen products. Here's what we got:

Whirlpool Microwave model WMH1162XVQ

Whirlpool Stove model GFG461LVQ

Whirlpool Dishwasher model GU2300XTVQ

Whirlpool Refrigerator model GB2FHDXWQOD

I finally got everything installed. The fridge I know was assembled in the USA. The microwave I know is from China. The dishwasher and range I am still unsure about. I'll have to check the serial numbers online or something. But so far, everything is working great. [3]

The stove conversion from natural gas to propane was a bit exhausting. I set off our CO2 detectors twice. Not good. But now that I've done everything properly, we're much better. I chose not to heed the fireman's advice to hire a professional... Hind sight, maybe I should have, but what's done is done. [4]

Now that is working properly, it is most impressive. It has two "Power burners" which cook and boil very fast. I highly recommend the convection option to anybody looking to buy. Everything cooks faster and much more evenly. [5]

The fridge is great because it holds everything with room for the kitchen sink... literally! And it boasts that it takes less energy than 1 light bulb to run.

The microwave is just like any other. Pops a bag of popcorn in 2:30. It cooked up some baked (nuked) potatoes pretty well and there's room in there for 2 full size dinner plates. [6]

The dishwasher has more buttons that I know what do with. It's got a "Power Scour" option that blasts water out of jets in the back. Great for when I cook on the "Power Burner" and burn the food on the bottom of the pan. [7]

I installed everything by myself with a little help from my wife and daughter for holding and attaching parts, and a friend of mine helped check my electrical wiring (I had to install a new plug for the microwave). Oh, and the fire department helped clear out the CO2. Everything was fairly straight forward and it probably took less than a dozen trips to Lowe's for the right parts.

I don't expect any problems, but if anything goes wrong, I will announce it here.

Until next time, please continue to buy American products. Avoid foreign junk as much as possible. Let's build this great country back up and get Americans honest jobs. And thank you for all you do. God Bless!

February 11 Update
1. As a quick aside… Yes, Valentine's Day is corny. And although it's supposed to be something to show you love to each other, it generally comes down on the man to do something nice versus the other way around. But is it really so bad to do something "extra" special just one time in February?
2. It still makes me sick thinking about all the people running out and buying those little hearts. I've since seen other brands that are made in the USA, but make sure you read the bag… If it's not made in USA, don't put it in your kid's mouth.
3. It turns out that both my dishwasher and range were made in the USA… Only one problem. In 2012, a lot of Whirlpool manufacturing plants started moving elsewhere. I'll continue telling you about my appliances since it's already been written, but before you go out and buy one, check the current manufacturer. Additionally, write them and tell them to quit sending American jobs somewhere else unless you're selling it to the same nation. Without American workers, people can't afford to buy it if they don't have to jobs to make the money.
4. Yes, the fire department came to the house… I thought the whole thing set up just fine until we tried using the broiler… Apparently, the broiler has another gas feed that needed to be adjusted. I changed out the regular oven feed, the stovetop burner feed, but I forgot the broiler. A few days later, the CO_2 detectors started playing their song. I called the fire department and they came out and cleared everything for us—at no charge. Those men that came that night were some of the most polite and professional men I have ever dealt with. I apologized for making them come all the way out to my place, but they told me it was no trouble and to call again if I don't feel my family is safe. Thank you!
5. Long term update… I no longer own the house that I installed this stove in and so I don't use the stove anymore. My wife and I used this stove for years before moving though. It was, by far, the best stove I have ever owned or used. It heated consistently and evenly. It was fairly easy to keep clean (a big problem when I cook). I wish I would have taken it with me.
6. I really like the size of this microwave, but honestly, the only reason I got a new one to begin with was to match the rest of the appliances in the kitchen. There was really nothing special (other than the size) about the microwave. It worked well and worked until we left. No complaints.
7. It seems that there is no such thing as a dishwasher that actually cleans "everything" you put in it. This dishwasher, with the "power scour" option,

worked well, but every once in a while, there was still some grime on the dishes. I'm not the type of person who cleans the dishes before putting them in the dishwasher. I'll put in plates, pots, pans, glasses, and silverware fully dirty. It certainly works better than the one I have now, but it wasn't perfect.

February 15, 2010

Last week, President Obama signed into law an increase of our nation's debt. Basically what that means is that we, as a nation, can borrow more money. Think of it this way. Since you're almost maxed out on your credit card, the credit card increased your spending limit. The worst part about this is that our children and our children's children will have to pay back our irresponsible spending. [1]

Do you know who owns our debt? You bet! China is our biggest lender... Oh, it gets better.

Sun Tzu said that the best strategy is to render an opponent helpless even before the battle begins. I'm not saying that China is our opponent or vice versa, but I don't think it's wise that China essentially controls what we can or cannot buy with the dollar in our pocket. Especially if we're over here "poking the bear."

Last month, President Obama decided to sell $6.4 billion in weapon systems to Taiwan... a move that China declared will "cause seriously negative effects" on the cooperation between the US and China.

Are we having fun yet 'cause I'm not done! Two colonels in China's army wrote a book titled "Unrestricted Warfare." It describes how a country like China could defeat a country with a superior military, like the United States. How? By using a variety of economic means to put the opponent in a position that castrates their military. [2]

On top of that, China has been vigorously modernizing its military force. Let's not forget that China is already a nuclear superpower.

Let me sum up... China is the largest foreign controller of the value of the American dollar. China literally wrote the book on how to defeat a superior military by means of controlling the American dollar. Do you see the connection?

Give America A Chance

Now many people speculate that China wouldn't dare take action since it stands to lose billions of dollars. Good point. What would cause them to want to lose that kind of revenue? Country and military pride? If we used the loans from China to help grow the military strength of their enemy, do you think there's a chance they would stop our economic ability? You bet!

There's no easy way to put this... We need to lessen our foreign dependence. We need to be more of a self-sufficient nation. Can we do that by buying American-made shoes? Not really. But it's a start. We need to stop buying foreign made products with money lent from foreign companies. It's like using a cash advance on your Visa card to pay your Visa bill. Sure, you're out of trouble this month, but in the long run, you're a whole lot worse off. [3]

Now, a change in subject (but not really). The number one reason people fail to quality for military service is obesity. Add criminal records, drug use, and lack of high school diplomas and we've got a serious problem... another one.

Did you know part of the reason the school lunch program was started was because so many of our youth were too malnourished to qualify for the military? We needed a strong, healthy, military in order to stay a free country then, and we need it now. This isn't the schools' problem, it's yours and it's mine.

We can't forget that there are those who threaten this country. Whether it be economic, military force, or terrorism, people want to destroy this great nation. If we want our grandchildren to have what we have, we have to take a stance. We have to quit buying their throw-away products and buy quality American-made merchandise. We have to quit eating 2,000 calorie cheeseburgers and teach our children how to cook healthy meals at home. This isn't a matter to be taken lightly; our national security should be our highest priority. [4]

Where do you draw the line? What is your stance? [5]

February 15 Update

1. I told you that February 15 would bring up some history repeating itself issues. Back when I started editing this book we were in another "crisis" where we needed to raise the debt limit. This is something that will continue to go on and on and on and on and on. It's getting to the point where it's ridiculous.
2. They literally wrote the book, people!
3. We didn't get into this debt with one person in one day. We got into this debt through the choices of millions over several years. It's not going to be an easy or quick change, but it is a change that we need to make. Alone, I can't even scratch the surface. Together, we can pull out of this debt and make our country rich.
4. I don't know about you, but I want my kids to have it better than I could have dreamed. I want my grandchildren to have it even better. If you want anything else, move to some other country and ruin their nation. Don't be a leech in this nation. Work, get paid, spend your money here, put somebody else to work. And take care of your kids. Feed them well.
5. I am drawing a line in the sand right now. I am standing on the side of the minority, but I want to change that. If you won't join me, fine, I'll do it without you. If you will join me, congratulations, you are on the side of the winners. America will be great again. We will do better than prosper, we will succeed!

March 3, 2010

Wow, has it been 2 weeks since I've last written? My excuse is pure business. Let me start off with the more mundane and move into the exciting stuff.

First of all, my new Whirlpool dishwasher. I'm a guy. And guys, you know how well we load dishwashers. We cram every dish, pot, pan, spoon, cup, and tool possible being certain no gap is left exposed. In doing so, it takes 2 cycles to get the dishes clean. I mentioned to my wife that I'm not sure it's any better than the old one to which she quickly replied, "Yes it is!" Continuing, she said "for what we paid, it's a whole lot better." I suppose that while purchasing new expensive stuff, its tough admitting that it's no better than the old, but then again, I am using cheap detergents and filling it too full. We'll see what happens with better detergent. (1)

Also I'm one of those guys who enjoys wearing a tie to work… I've got lots of ties, but years ago, my dad got me a few Rush Limbaugh collection ties. They're also the only ties that I get complimented on every time I wear one. Today, somebody walked and asked me if it's made in the USA. I'm proud to say that it is. If you're the type of guy who wears ties to work, likes vivid and loud colors, and likes compliments, you have to get some. (2)

Now for some exciting news. We bought a puppy last weekend. We hopped in the truck and drove about 13 hours round trip to get a 9-week old silver Labrador. So now comes the fun part of getting food dishes, training supplies, treats, and toys. Here's what we found…

Kong products, great for active chewers, made in the USA.

Crock Heavyweight bowls from Van Ness Plastics, Wal-Mart, made in the USA.

For food, I like Science Diet. It's made in the USA and has not been recalled since I've been using it.

This is my 3rd Labrador and all have been healthy, strong, and active. By the way, the Labrador… Made in the USA! [3]

Now for the really exciting news. We're going to have a baby! Last week, we found out that my wife is pregnant. So now, I get to talk about all the baby clothes and furniture we get, but that's a few months off. I'll have finished my one-year attempt at buying all-American products, so with any luck, this book will be published before the baby is born, but who knows, maybe I'll blog my continued attempts and successes. Obviously, I'm not going to give up buying American-made products. This country needs the revenue now more than ever. [4]

For now, thank you for your independent quests for all-American products and putting this country to work. Until next time, God bless and good night.

One last note I almost forgot about. I picked up a book at the public library. "The Caveman's Pregnancy Companion, A Survival Guide for Expectant Fathers," by David Port and John Ralston. So far, it's been quite entertaining. It is also, of course, made and printed in the USA.

March 3 Update

1. I think that's enough about dishwashers… The most important thing isn't the dishwasher itself; but the fact that there are dishwashers still made in the USA. Quality American-made products are out there. Don't let anybody tell you we don't make things here anymore.
2. I still wear the Rush ties every once in a while, but not as often anymore. My current job puts me in front of people quite a bit as an instructor… I want to look nice and I want to look professional, but I don't want to distract from the material I'm trying to teach. Rush ties can be distracting.
3. Apparently, I was incorrect in my statement that Science Diet hasn't been recalled… There was a recall in 2007 according to the FDA archive website. I still like it and I still use it, though.
4. Well, I didn't get this book published before the birth of my first son. And, I didn't get it published before the birth of my second son. The idea of going back and adding an updated commentary to my original commentary wasn't part of the plan. Between life and the things that happen in life, this book got shelved for a few years. It wasn't until discussing it with friends at work that it came back off the shelf. The update was necessary, so here we are.

The Rants and Raves of an American Patriot

March 11, 2010

First off, I apologize for my last writing. Even I feel like it was nearly incoherent writing, but then again, that was part of the purpose of writing in the first place. It seems quite a bit has happened lately, but I don't really know how to put it all in words.

Let me start off with some follow up, starting with my Whirlpool dishwasher. We bought some Target brand liquid dishwasher detergent. It is made in the USA. We've tried it in the past and it worked well with our old dishwasher. It works really well with the new one. I've been packing it as full as it gets and then some. With quality detergent, it works quite well.

The puppy, Hank, is doing pretty good. I've been working on getting him potty trained. Apparently, boys are a little tougher than girls. My older lab, Audi, was potty trained almost immediately. Hank, on the other hand, is taking some time. He's actually sitting with me today as I write. [1]

We haven't got him registered yet, but his official name will be "Saint Handkerchief Goober." He's got a white cross on his chest, hence the "Saint." My daughter has been reading "Hank the Cowdog" series of books which are very entertaining. And he has a tendency, when trying to get up stairs and other objects bigger than him, to collapse like a pile of goo. So Handkerchief Goober seemed fitting. [2]

And finally, most importantly, my pregnant wife. She is doing great. In a sort of cliché act, we bought a huge jar of pickles from Sam's Club. She has been craving soup lately and has actually put chopped up dill pickles in "spaghetti soup." Interesting to say the least.

One of the nice things about this book is that it gives me an outlet to talk about the baby. We've told family and a few friends, but for the most part, we're keeping it secret until we get a doctors confirmation. That doesn't happen until the 25th, but man am I excited! We started planning out the bedroom to make room for the crib, along with all the other details.

Part of the reason for suddenly getting a puppy was so that we can get him trained and replace the carpet. Finding American-made carpet should be fun.

We've also started our garden. It's a bit early to get things in the ground, but we started some seeds indoors and I picked up a bunch of local herbs from the nursery. Having plants growing in the house is a nice break from a long winter. I also got a couple dozen pots for house plants. The real cheap ones from Home Depot and Lowe's are made in the USA. The more expensive ones were from China. Of course, we got the American products.

Also, I've been looking for a water bottle made in the USA. Target had some "Nalgene" water bottles that have "Made in USA" clearly printed on the front of the bottle. Both my daughter and I got some. [3]

I've been wanting to make some quick emergency kits with band aids, matches, and other necessities to put in our cars. I think the Nalgene water bottles will make perfect kits for them. They're water tight and can be used for a number of purposes. When I get a kit together, I'll let you know what I put in them. It's always nice to be prepared for small emergencies. [4]

I pray all is well with you and yours. I've got so much to write, but time is so short.

March 11 Update

1. My goodness... Hank took forever to get fully potty trained. I don't know if it was the difference between boy/girl or if Audi was just that good of a dog, but they're completely different in every way. Hank is a good dog, but he was very slow in many ways.
2. Saint Handkerchief Goober is still a fitting name. The brightest bulb in the lamp, he's not... but as far as letting kids and babies crawl on him, he's perfect. He just pulls out his "goo" mentality and lays there while kids push, pull, and climb on him. There was a time when my oldest son was standing at the kitchen counter looking taller than normal. I asked what he was standing on, to which he replied, "Hank." When I walked around the counter, sure enough, he was standing on Hank's head. Hank was just lying there like goo, taking the punishment. Good dog, Hank!
3. I've still got my Nalgene water bottle and I take it to work every day. Although the label has scrubbed off from usage, it's still a bottle and comes with my highest recommendation as long as it's still made here. Anywhere else, don't buy it.
4. There are literally thousands of items you could stick in your water bottle, and, after thinking about it for a while, I can't give you a one size fits all listing. For me, with a few kids and general needs, I prefer band-aids, alcohol wipes, small candies/cough drops, and more band-aids. However, your needs could be completely different.

Give America A Chance

March 16, 2010

I want to take just a moment to talk about something I have heard about lately. For you, the reader, this will obviously be in the past... the self-executing bill. [1]

Here's my take on the topic... UNCONSTITUTIONAL!!!

First, let me tell you more about my politics. I know I said I didn't want to earlier, but I feel it has some play here. I am not political. I do not like politics. Call me crazy, but I believe that a bill should pass the way our Constitution set it up to pass. Or FAIL the way our Constitution set it up to fail. When you start passing bills that haven't been voted on, that's wrong! Many have speculated that the Senate already passed the bill. In some ways, that's true. The Senate passed a health care bill, but it's changed. Heck, it's totally different.

Imagine this. Let's say you and I vote on the "Pay A.J. $10 a Day Bill." Now in this bill, I propose to give you $15 a day and you pay me $10 a day. Would you vote yes? Of course you would. Now after you vote yes and it passes, I change it and say that I pay you nothing and you still owe me $10 a day. HECK NO! you say... Too bad, you already voted yes. I take the "Pay A.J. $10 a Day Bill" to some other people and encourage them to vote yes because I promise to share that $10 a day with them. All of a sudden, we've unanimously voted yes and the bill passes. Too bad, so sad for you. [2]

Like I said, I'm not a politics person so I may be way over-simplifying this, but whether it's a simple 10 bucks or a multi-billion dollar bill, it's still the same cowardly, underhanded tactics.

If the politicians are correct who say that Americans want this bill, write it up, debate it for the world to see, and pass it constitutionally. After all, Congressmen and Senators should listen to the people who vote for them, right? Isn't that what it means to be a Republic? You do remember the old saying, "And to the Republic for which it stands," don't you? [3]

Now for something a little more along the lines of the purpose for this book. Earlier at supper, my daughter humorously blurted out, "Hey, do you know where this pan was made?" She was referring to the pot and pan set my parents bought me years ago. I genuinely didn't know, so I asked. She replied that they were made in the USA. "See," she continued, "It says so right here." Right on the side of my Carico pan, it proudly stated "Made in the USA!"

I wish I could explain how much I love this country. I wish I could somehow share my patriotism with the world. This book is my attempt at just that. I want people to proudly remark just like my daughter did about the Carico pan. My countrymen made that pan. My countrymen have fought and died to uphold the Constitution of the United States. My country... well, it's your country too! Take pride in our values. Take pride in our people. Take pride in our Constitution and uphold it at all costs. [4]

Give America A Chance

March 16 Update

1. For the particular situation I'm referring to at this point (health care), the rule was shot down, but it's apparently been used more than a hundred times since it became a rule in the 1930's where it was used to maintain credit for the U.S. Government (sound familiar). It also makes a good out for Congressmen and Senators to deny their cooperation for a particular version of a bill (sound familiar). Just as a bit of education for you… If a bill gets passed as a self-executing bill and you voted for it… I don't care if it changed or not, you voted for it. If you don't want the blame, don't vote for it.
2. Well, wait a second, I kind of like this bill now. Remember, when I voted for it, I had planned on paying you more. It's not my fault that it got changed before others voted for it. It was "Bush's fault". That a bit of sarcasm for you.
3. Sometimes…rarely, but sometimes, I wish I was in politics so that I could try and clean house a little bit. Is it possible for an honest person to win an election anymore?
4. We truly have a great nation. It doesn't matter who you are or what your income is, you're much richer than many others across this planet. We live in the freest and best country on planet earth. Keep it that way!

March 22, 2010

Today, I'm frustrated with many things. Let me start off with the Census Bureau. I was a census enumerator for the 2000 census. I had just gotten out of the Air Force (the first time), I was jobless, and I needed some money. I understand the importance of the census for the most part, but a couple things still baffle me. [1]

Back in 2000, "Hispanic" wasn't considered a race. Many people were very frustrated with that. When I went door-to-door to people's houses and found people of Mexican descent, they were very upset when I told them they were supposed to check the "White" box. Some were extremely offended. Heck, I was offended that we were asking people for their race. [2]

Now, in 2010, the government has added a Hispanic check box but it is no less offensive. In 1790 (the first U.S. census), race was recorded because "Black" people were only counted as 3/5 of a person. Now, 220 years later, we're still asking the same questions. Why? Now I know the reason and it is no less offensive than counting any American as less than a whole person. It has to do with financial aid and voting boundaries. I, personally, find is extremely offensive and devaluing to every American individual. [3]

Another frustrating thing happened today (or should I say late last night when most Americans were sleeping peacefully). The infamous health care bill passed. In the words of the Tennessee Representative Marsha Blackburn "Freedom died a little bit yesterday. Unfortunately, some are celebrating." [4]

The United States government passed a bill that requires supposedly free Americans to buy a product… health insurance.

Could you imagine if the government required every American to by this book? Not only would it be ridiculous, but it would be illegal!

I joined the military to learn a trade. [5]

I went to college to earn a degree. [6]

I worked my butt off to be able to earn enough money to buy a house.

And I pay a lot of money to buy insurance for my family.

I took the bull by the horns in my pursuit of happiness and my blood, sweat, and tears earned every bit of happiness I earned. If you want to be a lazy bum, not work, not learn a trade, not go to college, and not pursue your own happiness, then DARNIT, you DON'T DESERVE IT!!!

Far be it from me to deny someone help, but that's my choice. You don't have the right to demand it from me. [7]

Fortunately, last I heard, 38 states are filing challenges to Obama's unconstitutional tyranny. Some states are filing challenges to the bill and others are filing so that the U.S. government can't force their illegal and immoral laws on their state. To those states, I say Thank You for standing up for what is right. [8]

If you want every American to have health insurance, provide them jobs. Here's where you come in. Yes, YOU! We can't provide jobs for Americans unless there's something to work for. We can't provide jobs for Americans unless there's someone to work for.

We, you and me, have to create a vacuum of products so American companies can hire more people to make those products and fill that void. I've said it over and over; we have to buy American products.

I've listed product after product in this book. Here's another one… Homz plastic storage bins… they're made in the USA and they only cost $4 at K-Mart. There's more out there and I won't find them all. It's up to you. Will you do your part? [9]

March 22 Update

1. I had to go door-to-door to "encourage" people to fill out their census forms. Sometimes, I would spend an hour or more in a person's home filling out the form for them. It was humiliating for me and for the people whose privacy I was invading. Not my proudest job.
2. The census provides a nice fine of $100 for not completing the census. It also provides a nice $500 fine for deliberately misstating information (lying) on the census form. On most forms, the race is a voluntarily… not so on the census. When I fill out most forms, I usually check Native American. My reasoning, I was born here. I am a native United States American. For the census, however, if you or I were to choose anything other than what "they" want you to "classify" yourself or myself, we could be subject to a fine.
3. How do we expect to get over the racial issues in this country when the highest law in the land can't get over it?
4. As we all know, the health care bill that was passed in 2010 wasn't the be-all, end-all. There were more votes and more bills passed taking more and more of our American freedoms.
5. I also served to proudly stand up for the rights of Americans. I still serve my country as a citizen of these United States and I still proudly stand up for the rights of Americans… all Americans.
6. I'm not a perfect student. Getting a college degree was a fight for me and that fight wasn't easy.
7. I believe in helping those who are downtrodden. I believe in helping those who truly need help. I do not believe in helping those who refuse to help themselves.
8. Unfortunately, time has proven that even those 38 states caved in.
9. I won't find them all because my personal needs don't encompass the entire spectrum of products. If you're a tool fanatic, let others know what tools are made in the USA. If you're a chef, let others know what cookware is made in the USA. If you're a plumber, or a carpenter, or an electrician, let others know what products in your field are made in the USA. You get the picture.

March 24, 2010

Just a quick note today… Much more fun and not as much preaching from my soapbox.

The other day, I went to start my Harley Davidson after a long, cold winter. To my dismay, however, it wouldn't start. It just made a clicking sound from somewhere in the fuse panel. I knew it wasn't the starter because I hadn't tried starting yet. So I located the clicking by feeling for which fuse or relay was shaking as it clicked. It was the system relay.

I finally made it up to O'Reilly Auto Parts earlier today and asked if they had a replacement. After about 5 minutes of searching the back shelves, the salesman came back with a new relay in a BWD Automotive box with "Made in China" stamped on it. I, of course, asked if he had any that were made in the USA. He told me that he had a cheaper one. I replied, "That's the one I want. It's probably made in the USA and better quality." A few seconds later, he came back to the counter with a grin. Sure enough, for 5 bucks ($4 cheaper), he had a MasterPro ignition relay switch with a beautiful, made in USA script on the side. Not only that, but the box was printed in the USA. How good can you get? [1]

Moral of the story… just because someone hands you a Chinese sub-product doesn't mean you have to take it. There are usually (not always) better alternatives. Thank you MasterPro, you made my day!

March 24 Update

1. At first, I found it surprising that American-made products were cheaper. Now, I know that it happens more often than not. This book is full of those examples. Don't take my word for it, though, try it for yourself.

Give America A Chance

April 7, 2010

It's been a couple weeks since I've last written. To my defense, I went to California for work for nearly a week. It was my first time in the Golden State. I did a little time in both Long Beach and San Diego. I didn't get a whole lot of "play" time, but I did get about an hour to tour the USS Midway. By the way, an hour is about 8 hours too short to get the full effect. For the most part, I was highly impressed.

The only unimpressive thing about the whole aircraft carrier was the gift shop. I stopped in to see if I could get something cool for my daughter. It was pretty much filled with the same Chinese junk you could get at any toy store. [1]

Besides that, there are a couple topics I'd like to discuss from recent news. Yesterday, President Obama announced the United States' new nuclear posture review. To say it plainly, it's a victory for our enemies. We've laid out the single greatest deterrent our country possesses. And we laid it out so foreign adversaries can walk all over us.

Quite simply, we won't update our arsenal. We won't threaten the use of a nuclear weapon unless we are first attacked by a nuke. Ralph Peters from the New York Post said it better than I ever could; "If a thug has a knife, but knows you're packing a gun, he's considerably less likely to attack you. Why promise him that you won't use the gun—and might not use your knife."

Enough said. [2]

Something else that frightens me is a proposal from a senator from West Virginia, Jay Rockefeller, and a senator from Maine, Olympia Snowe. Here's my fear... President Obama already owns many of our "so-called" private companies. He's done so via the cover of strengthening our nation. Now, our cyberspace is at risk of being controlled by our government. We live in a world where people use the internet from everything from buying groceries to communicating private medical information to our doctors.

The new proposal would create a "national cybersecurity advisor" that answers directly to the president. Scared yet? Rockefeller and Snowe say that the Cybersecurity Act of 2010 will empower owners to meet cybersecurity challenges. Because they don't already have that empowerment? Come on, you're not fooling anybody. I think we all see where this is heading... China anybody? [3]

Another thing (change in topic) that really chaps my hide is the whole scenario that most of us remember from years ago for the funeral of one of our fallen Marine hero's, Lance Corporal Matthew Snyder. That's the funeral where protestors preached profanity at Snyder's funeral. It was disgusting to say the least. Snyder's father rightfully sued and, at first, won the case. It has since been tossed out and now, Snyder's father has been court ordered to pay the sick protesters court bills. [4]

This court case will obviously continue, with the support of true Americans, but I have to ask why this happened in the first place. Our heroes in the military fight to defend free speech, but if anybody abuses that right screaming profanities during a painful funeral, it's gone too far. [5]

Unfortunately, I don't have the answers to these problems. I just know that some of the things happening in my country frighten and straight up disgust me. Just because you have the legal right to do something does not justify your actions. Legal or illegal, our morals should tell us what is right and wrong. [6]

Now stand up and do what's right.

April 7 Update

1. Why would a US National museum be full of foreign junk? We have got to stop this dependence on foreign-made products. We know they're not safe, we know they're not beneficial to our country, so why can't we spend a bit more time to find good American products to fill a great American museum?
2. It's not even tough to understand. Why would you carry a weapon? To protect yourself, right? Would you carry that weapon with a sign that says you won't use it unless they use their first? In some situations, that means you won't use your weapon until it's too late to use your weapon. I think most Americans understand that our nuclear weapons are designed for a mutual destruction scenario. If you launch against us, we're going to destroy you. That's understood, but it's not the rule. Why would you tell the enemy our rule? Wouldn't it be better for our enemies to question, even a little bit, whether or not we'll attack them first if they even start rising up against American citizens?
3. If you have internet, and you probably do, you probably have some sort of password protection on your account. It might be a low-level protection to keep the honest, honest or it might be a robust security designed to thwart even the most determined hacker, but you have the right to protect your cyber security, you have the empowerment already.

This act was re-introduced in 2013 and has not passed, but as we all know, history repeats itself. If we just sit by, it will eventually get enacted.
4. I'm not going to name the group that protested at the funeral because I don't support anything they do and I certainly don't support what name they hide behind.
5. In 2011, the Supreme Court voted against Snyder in support of free speech. They basically said that the sicko's weren't protesting Snyder's funeral, rather issues of the United States in general. It was a sad day.
6. There are a lot of things that I have the legal right to do. That doesn't mean that it's right.

April 15, 2010

Happy tax day everybody! Are you excited? Well, you should because chances are, you're paying less taxes this year than you will next year. Oh, I know President Obama said not to worry... I hate to break it to you, but the only thing Obama is good at is politics. And politics = lies. Don't believe me, well come this time next year, you will. [1]

Anyway, I don't want to talk about taxes. I want to talk about a few American-made products. Earlier this week, my daughter turned 8 years old. We threw her a little party on Saturday and went to the zoo with friends on Sunday.

My wife picked up some cool party plates and napkins that were, of course, made in the USA. She got a brand called "Creative Converting" out of Oshkosh, WI. [2]

Also, earlier this week, we went to a local drug sore to see if we could get a cool mist humidifier. It was recommended for moms-to-be. We found a Vicks Cool Mist Humidifier made by KAZ Incorporated out of Hudson, NY. Believe it or not, it too was made in the USA.

As a bonus, we also came across Kid K'Nex building blocks that were also made in the USA. We got them for upcoming birthdays.

You know, sometimes I get so excited when I find American-made products that I can't keep my mouth shut, hence the book. But I catch myself at work doing the same thing. I'll be talking to somebody about anything and instantly, without thinking about it, I'll start picking things up off of other people's desks to see where it was made. Water bottles, lunch boxes, toy trinkets... Nine times out of ten, it's junk made in China. And when I bring up the fact, I usually get some sort of lame excuse: "Oh, well

I just needed something quick," or "I never even checked." But if it's an American-made product, I get an excited, "That's right!" [3]

Most people are patriotic about the USA and proud of our products, they just don't bother to check. Which is part of the purpose of this book... check your labels, people!

By the way, everything seems to be going smoothly with my wife's pregnancy. No major morning sickness or illnesses. We had our first doctor's appointment last Monday and they gave us an ultrasound picture. The baby is about the size of a peanut and expected to arrive on November 10th. [4]

We've been looking at American-made bottles, pacifiers, and such and have been fairly successful, but I don't want to write about them until we actually get them and I can testify to their quality. [5]

I really do love this country. The people, the landscape, the opportunities, but most of all, I love the freedom. I, along with so many others, will do whatever it takes to keep that freedom. I am willing, are you? [6]

April 15 Update

1. Turns out, I was only partially correct. The tax rates didn't actually go up, but the marginal tax brackets didn't go up as much as it should have either. For example, let's say that you and your spouse made $65,000 in 2008. At a 15% marginal rate, you would have brought home $55,250. In 2009, the marginal rate income bracket raised 4%. Which means if you also made a 4% pay raise, you would have made $67,600 and, at a 15% marginal rate, you would have brought home $57,460. In 2010, however, the marginal rate income bracket did not even raise 1%. If you got your traditional 4% pay raise you would have made $70,300, but you would have been bumped into the 25% marginal rate making your take home pay only $52,728. That's a "loss" of $4,732 from 2009. If it feels like you took home less pay, you probably did.

   You would have actually been better off passing on the pay raise and staying in the 15% tax bracket.

   As an aside, the marginal rate only increased about 1.5% in 2011, 2.5% in 2012, and 2.5% in 2013.

2. I am surprised at the amount of party supplies at the local dollar stores that are made in the USA. Check it out for yourself. They're usually a whole lot cheaper than the grocery store, and they're made in the USA. Cheaper and better, great combination.

3. It's interesting that people feel the need to defend buying foreign products, but not for buying American-made products. Guilty conscience?

4. He came early... Jonah was born on November 4th at 10lbs 6oz. He was a big boy!

5. There were a few products we used for our babies and still use for them today as toddlers. Starting off, we used NUK brand "plugs" (pacifiers) for Jonah. They're made in Germany, but it's better than the alternative. For Caleb, he wanted nothing but Soothies, which are made in USA.

   For bottles, we found some Gerber and NUK bottles that were made in USA (NUK had some German parts).

   In all honesty, it wasn't that tough to find American-made products for our kids once we started looking in the right places. Unfortunately, some of the "big-box" stores carry the junk that I won't put in my kids mouth.

   As a quick fun note, we found Constructive Eating utensils for the kids... Check them out, especially for your boys!

6. Quite simply, are you a Patriot?

Give America A Chance

April 21, 2010

I was in the Air Force for a while and one thing always bothered me... Could I ever be asked to target Israel as an enemy? I had no real reason to wonder such a thing, and it never caused me to lose sleep at night, but it was there...right along with the fears of enforcing martial law on my own countrymen. [1]

I know many of my fellow airmen felt the same way. But today, an airman asked a very similar question to the Chairman to the Joint Chief of Staff, Adm. Mike Mullen. This airman was concerned about Israel taking the Iran nuclear issue into their own hands and attacking Iran by way of Iraq. Iraq is currently a "no-fly" zone enforced by our hero's in that country. The airman asked if the US would shoot down Israeli jets flying through Iraq.

Years ago, pre-Obama, the answer would have been a resounding, No! Heck, we probably would have escorted and helped them be successful.

Now, however, I'm not so sure... And neither is Adm. Mullen apparently. He pulled a political play and sideswiped the question. Even when the airman asked a second time, more directly, whether he could ever be given the order to attack our closest ally, Mullen couldn't, or wouldn't, answer the question. [2]

Since I like analogies, imagine this... Imagine the guy who lives behind you was lobbing stones via a test catapult. He is openly trying to create a catapult system that would destroy your best friend's home and family. As he gets closer and closer to success, your best friend gets aggravated and worried. He decides that one night, he is going to sneak in and destroy their catapult. But, he has to go through your property which is clearly marked with "NO TRESPASSING" signs. If one night, you see your friend moving through your property with the intention of destroying the aggressor's catapult, would your use force to stop him?

I wish it was more complicated than that, but it isn't. I have my answer, you have yours. Maybe it's different, maybe it's not. The problem is, our military leaders can't or won't answer that question. Why not? [3]

Now a change in topic. Today I went to our local Barnett Harley Davidson to get a new battery. I forgot to charge mine all winter and now it's dead. I chose to go with the more expensive Harley Davidson brand for one simple reason… It's made in the USA. While I was there, I mentioned that I looked at cheaper brands and questioned why I should go the HD route. His answer was simple. I could have gone with a cheaper brand, and it would've worked fine, but they're not made in the USA. Point taken. [4]

Last weekend, we had friends over for dinner. Everybody brought something, but one thing caught my eye. One of our friends brought a Marie Callender's Razzleberry Pie. After everybody left and we were cleaning up, I picked up the pie box to throw it away, but I noticed a small American flag in the corner. Under the flag were the words, "Proudly made in the USA." Whether he bought it for that or not, I don't know, but it made me think… well of course it was made in the USA, who would buy a pie made in China?

Obviously, other countries make pie, but China came to mind since we seem to be outsourcing most everything else there. Would you buy a pie that said, "Proudly made in China?" Think about that. [5]

Give America A Chance

April 21 Update

1. I don't know if anybody reading this follows any of the conspiracy theories or not, but I like to check them out every once in a while. In fact, I give them about the same credibility as I do to FOX or CNN. Both blow things way out of proportion for ratings.

    There's a lot of conspiracy rants lately about the government buying up thousands upon thousands of small arms ammunition. I heard it said that enough rounds have been bought to fight the Iraq and Afghanistan wars for another plethora of years, but they're not buying them for the military, they're buying it for DHS, USPS, etc. This makes many wonder about the potential for a looming martial law. I don't have a thought on the matter one way or the other, but I do have the fear.

2. That frightens me a little bit… Maybe it frightens me a lot. There are people out there who believe that Israel shouldn't be a nation because they took it via war. With that mentality, America shouldn't really be a country either… or Taiwan, or Tibet, or a number of other countries. Fact is, Israel is a nation and it is an American ally. Period.

3. I still don't think it's much more difficult than that. As the year progressed, I tend to think more and more that many of our nation's leaders would shun Israel for taking such an action. In my eyes, that's a problem.

4. One thing I've tried over and over to express is that American-made products are out there, they're better, and they're usually cheaper. In this particular case, the battery wasn't. I'm sure I could have found an alternative brand made in the USA for cheaper, but as all HD riders want HD equipment, I wanted to keep my resale value high. Another thing HD riders know is that in addition to Harley Davidson, HD also stands for hundred dollars. If you tack an HD logo on something, the price just went up a hundred dollars.

5. Got you thinking, didn't I?

April 25, 2010

Nothing too dramatic to discuss, but I wanted to mention some more quality products. Earlier this week, we headed out in search of an American-made cultivator. I was looking for one of those hand tools that you just roll back and forth to tear up the soil. Whether it is the time of year or just lack of popularity, I couldn't find a single quality hand cultivator. But that's not what I want to talk about… I want to talk about what I did find.

At Harbor Freight of all places, I came across a Harbor Freight brand FLATFREE wheelbarrow tire. I've been looking for one, but they're all Chinese, at least the ones at my usual stores. Harbor Freight was about 10 bucks less and made in the USA. [1]

I was also on the hunt for paint and painting supplies. I came across Wooster brand paint supplies for extremely cheap. The roller, two pads, roller pan, and disposable liners ran me about 15 bucks at Home Depot. And of course, they all have "Made in the USA" proudly written on them.

To make a great weekend better, I got a haircut earlier tonight. My wife cuts my hair and we use a set of clippers I've had for years. They're a great, dependable set of Oster brand clippers. For the first time, I noticed that they're made in the USA. I love it when I find out I bought American-made products long before I really even cared. [2]

So I had a great, productive weekend. I hope you did too. Keep on buying American-made products. Now, more than ever, your country needs you.

April 25 Update

1. I knew Harbor Freight sells some cheap stuff (price-wise), but I had no idea that some of their merchandise was made in the USA. Harbor Freight was a last ditch effort (I was getting sick and tired of filling the original tire every time I wanted to use the wheelbarrow). I guess I shouldn't be surprised so much anymore. American-made, quality merchandise is everywhere... You just have to look.
2. Those clippers lasted me until about a year ago when we received a new set of Wahl clippers, also made in the USA. Nothing against Oster, American-made clippers, they served me well, but they were old. In fact, I think I bought it used sometime in the late 1990's.

April 29, 2010

I live less than an hour's drive from the most dangerous city in the world. Since I've lived here, my family has been run off the road, threatened personally by a man pointing a gun at us (same person), and was within a few feet of a drive-by shooting. Now I don't personally know any of the gun-toting crazies that put my family in danger, but we have been in danger!

I live about 35 miles from Juarez, Mexico. Why are they the most dangerous city in the world? 1,600 murders last year. From press reporting, they're going to pass that easily this year. I'm not going to claim that the situations my family has been involved in was spillover from the Mexican violence; I just added that to put my city, that I feel safe in, in comparison. Warning, ranting just ahead!

Arizona recently decided to enforce a federal law regarding Mexican citizens illegally entering our country. Do you want to know something else that's crazy? They also enforce the seatbelt law. You see, when you enter the United States illegally or forget to wear your seatbelt when you're driving; you have broken a law that was established by a United States government. You should already know where I'm going with this. If not, read on…

I, however, have a problem with one of those laws. One of those laws protects me from myself while the other protects our nation from illegal activity.

Let me side track for a moment. I ride a motorcycle. In the state of New Mexico, I can choose whether or not I want to wear a helmet. 99% of the time, I wear a helmet. Why? Because I choose to protect myself. Even before seatbelts were a federal law, I chose to protect myself by wearing a seatbelt. Believe it or not, I also choose to cook my Thanksgiving turkey, keep my eyes open when I walk across the street, and wash my hands after using the bathroom. Not because it's the law, but because I choose to protect myself from myself.

I do not have the right to sit across the border from the most dangerous city in the world and capture or kill people trespassing. For that, I am forced to rely on my state, local, and federal government. I feel safe in my city because I expect my state, local, and city government to stop illegal activity. Heck, I pay my taxes to ensure they do so.

Arizona, however, has decided openly that they are going to do what their taxpayers pay them to do. Instead of cheering and applause of gratitude, idiots from both sides of the US/MX border are protesting and chastising them. You should be chastising your law enforcement officers if they are not upholding the law! [1]

Imagine for a second you were walking into your local Wal-Mart when a group of gun-toting idiots accidently shot your wife or child in a drive-by shooting. Later on, you come to find out that these gun-toting idiots were illegal immigrants from Mexico who were after a local drug pusher who stole money from the illegal gun-toting idiots.

Are you following me yet?

Now imagine you're a rancher in Arizona who was just killed by illegal immigrants who were trying to sneak drugs into your country across your property. Ahhh, now you remember. [2]

So since I, or you, can get arrested for refusing to wear a seatbelt while driving to the Piggly Wiggly for milk and eggs, shouldn't an illegal immigrant be arrested or entering our country illegally?

But you say, "We need the immigrants for cheap labor. They do the jobs Americans refuse to do." That's a load of bull and you know it! We, as Americans are, generally, a hard working nation. Sure, we've got some lazy slobs who refuse to do work that is "beneath them," let 'em starve.

I've lived a lot of places where illegal workers aren't a problem. I've personally done the jobs some lazy slobs say are beneath them. Besides, if some junk companies are paying illegal workers less than they're worth, isn't that slave labor? Where's the anger in that? I don't buy the load of bull that we need illegal workers. If a company can't make it by paying a fair salary to their workers, let them fail. Harsh? Yes! Fair? Yes! [4]

If you don't agree with our immigration laws, then write your congressmen and ask them to change it. Don't criticize the law enforcement officers who are paid to enforce our laws. I don't agree with the seatbelt law, but I'm not out forming protests groups threatening to punish any state that enforces it. That's ridiculous! It's a crying shame to see people trying to punish Arizona for enforcing laws that we, as a nation, or even we, as a state, have decided upon.

But then you say, "We were all immigrants once." Yes, but my ancestors did so legally. As do many Mexican immigrants every single day. You say, "Most illegal immigrants are law abiding citizens." Does the word illegal mean anything to you? If I go to Mexico illegally, I would rightfully get arrested. Why is it different the other way around? [5]

Listen, Americans need those jobs. Americans need work. We've got an unemployment problem that is out of control. If a licensed, legal immigrant wants to work in the US, so be it. But he or she has to uphold the same laws that you and I have to abide by. I'm not against immigration, I'm against illegal immigration. And I'm against you if you say that anybody can enter my country and disobey our laws. We are America, we are Americans! If you choose any other country first, then get out and show your pride elsewhere. I don't care about the color of your skin. I don't care about your past. I care about your allegiance to the United States of America. So you don't agree with all of our laws, fine! I don't either. But do you obey our laws? Do you care about your fellow Americans? Did your ancestors enter this country legally? Are you an advocate of American freedom? [6]

I AM AN AMERICAN!!! Are you? [7]

April 29 Update

1. Why is this so hard for people to understand?
2. In case you don't remember, a US citizen was murdered on his own property by people crossing the US/MX border illegally. They were crossing illegally to sell illegal drugs. Lots of laws broken there, starting with crossing the border illegally. Somebody should really put a stop to that, huh?
3. I'm not trying to sound like a jerk, but I really believe in enforcing the laws that we put in place. There may come a time when I will simply say enough is enough, but most of the laws we have in place right now aren't half bad.

    I get annoyed when people tell me that we need illegal immigrants to do janitorial work or mundane labor. I think that's plain racist.
4. If I knew an American company was employing illegal workers, I would stop buying from them in a second (Ah hem, Wal-Mart, you've been busted a few times, haven't you?).
5. If most illegal immigrants are law abiding citizens, then why do they hide when law enforcement comes around? Oh, I know!!! It's because they're not law abiding citizens. They broke the law coming into our country.

    I've got an idea floating around in my head that just might solve our immigration problem. I'll bet a thousand other Americans do as well. So why can't the "smart" people that we elect, solve the problem?
6. I half-heartedly apologize for such a long rant, but c'mon America, get your act together. We were founded on the ability to provide opportunities to the needy, to the hungry, to the disheartened. The problem lies in our policymakers. Democrats sort of want illegal immigrants because they've fooled the public into thinking that democrats actually care for them. Republicans don't want illegal immigrants because they'll lose their status as politicians by getting voted out.

    If Americans knew the real person behind the politician, nobody would want you.

    Democrats, you're just a bunch of rich millionaires who have fooled the world, but you don't actually give a rats behind about the "little people" you trample on to get into office. Your donation history makes that abundantly clear. Republicans in office routinely donate more of their own money to help the needy.

    Republicans, you're just a bunch of business owners who can't wait to see the "bottom line" dollar figure. There's a reason people think there's more millionaire republicans than democrats... it's not because it's true (since it isn't), it's because at the end of the day, you want to know what something costs.

Do either of you really care about the people?

7. I am not a democrat. I am not a republican. I am an American!

    I truly believe the American people would vote significantly differently if we could rid ourselves of the democrat/republican labels. Quit hiding behind your label and do something for your country! We're broke. We're hurting. We need strong leadership. And I'm afraid we won't find it in my lifetime. It's a shame really.

Give America A Chance

May 2, 2010

I don't want to be an "I told you so," so I won't. Instead, let me tell you a little story...

A deputy in Arizona is on a patrol when he comes across a large amount of illegal drugs hidden near a highway. In addition to the deputy finding drugs, a group of armed men found the deputy. The armed men shot the deputy. Unfortunately, this story is true. Fortunately the deputy is going to be ok.

Here are some more facts; the drugs that were stashed were illegal marijuana. The deputy was shot by an assault rifle. The drugs were stashed away in an area known to be a drug-smuggling corridor. And although the five men were not captured, they were Hispanic, possibly (although not known) illegal drug smugglers from Mexico. (1)

Now normally, I don't like to throw in the race card and point out that the men were Hispanic. I did that for a couple of reasons.

First, the emphasis that the Hispanic men may have been illegal immigrants. Illegal border crossing has to be stopped whether the illegals are drug smugglers or otherwise law-abiding citizens who are just after a better life. (2)

I also pointed out that the deputy was shot by an assault rifle. I have nothing against assault rifles. In fact, many perfectly legitimate US citizens own assault rifles and shoot them responsibly. I don't think assault rifles should be banned any more than I (point 2) think Hispanics should be banned. Both points are ridiculous. (3)

Hispanics are an asset to this country along with every other ethnicity that has legally entered this country. Out melting pot society is part of what makes the United States of America so great.

What has to be stopped is illegal activity. If you are entering my country illegally for any reason, you are an outlaw and I will support any effort to stop you and get you out.

Now on to something else… the oil spill in the Gulf of Mexico. This, I feel, is very similar to the ranting I gave on April 29, 2010. The government has the responsibility to protect us from illegal activity. Let me add on to that, man-made disasters. [4]

The oil spill is a tragic man-made disaster. The U.S. government should have stepped in on day 1 to help contain and limit the effect on local wildlife. I don't know what role the government is taking, but I heard a press conference a couple days ago where someone asked when the government was going to take over. The answer baffled me… BP is doing a fine job. WHAT?

From day one, the government should have jumped in there and thrown everything they had at controlling that spill and sent the bill later. [5]

Now, we're over a week later, fish and birds are dying. Restaurants are losing their business. And the U.S. government says they're doing just fine???

We are still the greatest nation on planet earth, but I don't understand this current administration. Listen, Obama, if you're not up to the job, step aside and let a real leader take the reins. We're falling apart from the inside out, not the other way around. We need command executive leadership, and frankly, you don't show much change that I believe in.

It's time we, as Americans, dictate what we believe in. I don't think it's coming from a washed up community organizer. Rant over, good night! [6]

Give America A Chance

May 2 Update

1. Even as I type this up, I'm getting a little heated over my choice of words... Be patient with me. This isn't normally the way I'd like to write up a story.
2. Put plainly, legal immigrants don't cross a border illegally. That makes them illegal. If you're crossing illegally, there's probably a reason you aren't allowed to cross the border legally. Whatever the case, illegal activity is illegal.
3. I also don't think the Scottish, English, Russian, Chinese, or Africans, etc. should be outlawed. Before you start getting hot-headed calling me all sorts of names that probably aren't true, think of it this way... It's not the tool, the clothing, the person, the race, the sex, the "whatever" that I think should be outlawed, it's the illegal activity. Imagine that, a person who thinks that illegal activity should be outlawed.
4. Why would the government be responsible for protecting us from man-made disasters? Oh yea, because we pay taxes to them to handle some of those issues.
5. Imagine you had a fire in your yard that was spreading and threatening your neighbors. Would the fire department come out and look at the devastation and say, "well, you're doing a fine job with your garden hose, we'll stick this one out for a while?" Of course not, they'll come in with hoses bursting and if they find you at fault, they'll bill you. That's why we pay taxes. Unless, of course, the fire chief is corrupt, lazy, incompetent, or all of the above.
6. It's sad that I even have to say that "it's time we, as Americans, dictate what we believe in." Isn't that what our founding fathers had planned all along?

May 4, 2010

After a few days of my ranting, I feel it's a good idea to get on the other topic of this book... American-made products!

Years ago, I bought a Kenmore vacuum cleaner. I'm sure it was made in China, but I have sworn up and down that it's the best vacuum cleaner built... even today. I even put it head-to-head against a Kirby. Kenmore won hands down until it came to the attachments Kirby comes with—talk about turning a pistol into a Gatling gun, wow! [1]

Anyway, as with any vacuum, over time things wear out and bags need to be replaced. Yesterday, I picked up Kenmore vacuum cleaner bags and to my surprise, they were made in the USA! Like I said though... I'm sure the vacuum cleaner itself was made in China so rather than supporting the Chinese, support your local area and check pawn shops or put out a wanted ad.

Have you ever been to your local dollar store? It's like a flea market for new items. They usually have just about anything under the sun. Surprisingly, they also have a lot of American-made products. Unfortunately, spray bottles aren't one of them (at least not the one I went to). You know those fancy spray bottles that come in a multitude of colors... I bought one. Of course it was before I started writing this book, but it made me think... I bought the spray bottle for a sanitizing agent. It was a fancy blue bottle made in China that didn't work worth a lick. I remember thinking, "what good does it do me to put a food grade sanitizer in a Chinese plastic bottle." Luckily, it broke soon after.

The other day, however, I found spray bottles made in the USA! At my local Wal-Mart, they carry The Bottlecrew spray bottles. They work great, they're clear so I can

Give America A Chance

guess what's in them, and they have a special spot on the side to write so I don't have to guess. Even better, they were only 89 cents... No more worrying! [2]

I also picked up Husky brand garbage bags. I usually buy the no-name cheapo brand, but they were too ashamed to put where they were made. Husky brand bags were only a few pennies more expensive and are proud to say they were made in the USA. [3]

With a pregnant wife at home, we're hesitant to put carpet cleaner on the floor where she often walks barefoot. But with a new puppy that is only 97% potty trained, we have to. Resolve carpet cleaner, made in the USA, gives us much less reason to be hesitant. When the Chinese wear masks because even they don't want to breathe their air, I sure don't want that stuff floating around my home. [4]

Ok, awhile back, I promised to tell the good and the bad about our Whirlpool kitchen products. I've got a "bad." The drawer under the stove is junk. We use it to store baking pans and casserole dishes. Every time you pull it out, it gets stuck on the going back in. I suppose if that's the worse that happens, were in good shape. But if you want to buy a new stove solely for the bottom drawer, choose a different model. [5]

Well, I feel good today. No whining or ranting that I want to discuss. I think I can sleep in peace tonight and I pray that you do too. Thank you for being an awesome American. Together, we can make sure our children's children can sleep in peace at night too... Good night and God bless! [6]

May 4 Update

1. I don't have the vacuum cleaner anymore... It finally gave out after almost 15 years. I never checked to see where it was made... Maybe I didn't really want to know, but now I'm kicking myself because after a few minutes of online research, some Kenmore vacuum cleaners are made in the USA and others aren't. It would be interesting to know since most vacuum cleaners don't last 15 years... unless you buy a Kirby, but for almost $2,000 it better become a family heirloom to pass on to my kids. According to the Kirby website, all Kirby home care systems are made in America.
2. I actually still have one of these bottles left. I think I bought three when I first got them. The others just got beat up. The one that I have left is starting to get weak in the trigger, but I probably use it 3 or 4 times per week. Not bad for 89 cents.
3. Why wouldn't more companies proudly advertise where they're made? Either you're made in the USA or not. If you are, be proud of it and advertise it so Americans everywhere know that you are supporting your country. If you're not, keep trying to hide it so Americans can call you out and shame you. Sorry, but it's true.
4. Eventually, we just switched to using baking soda. Many brands are made in the USA and it does a pretty good job of absorbing the odors before vacuuming them up.
5. I was really hoping to avoid saying anything bad about my new appliances, but in the effort of honesty, I want to be completely up front. I don't have a problem calling out an American product if it doesn't meet my quality standards, but I'd prefer the company to just make a quality product.
6. A full day without a rant... Awesome!

Give America A Chance

May 6, 2010

OK, I'm in a good mood, so I don't want to rant much, but there are a couple stupid things I want to talk about. The principal and vice principal at Live Oak High School in Morgan Hill, CA and the Phoenix Suns basketball team. And yes, I believe I used "stupid" appropriately.

First off, Live Oak H.S. Some students wore clothing with the American flag on it yesterday... Yesterday was a school day... Yesterday was also May 5, 2010, or Cinco de Mayo for some. Is that a bad thing...No.? I don't even think this would be bad if you were in Mexico. The 5th of May does not announce an American victory; it was a Mexican/French battle victory for the Mexicans. But some students were told to change their clothing because it may be offensive to some Mexicans. [1]

Maybe it would have been offensive to wear a French flag in Mexico, but certainly not an American flag in America. Like I said... stupid!

Secondly, the Phoenix Suns wore shirts that said "Los Suns." That's kind of neat. They wore them on Cinco de Mayo. Fun, right? Well, they wore it in support of illegal immigration. Come on guys, you've got children watching you. Athletes are often looked up to by young impressionable kids and let's face it; most of the news isn't about athletes doing good for their communities. Now you're teaching them to break a Federal law. Stupid for so many reasons. [2]

And now, an awesome, semi-related topic. My wife went to the maternity store yesterday for new clothes. There was a maternity shirt that said "Made in the USA." My wife, an outright patriot, bought it. [3]

The sales clerks in the store apparently got a kick out of the shirt as well since they mentioned that they were afraid of the kickback they would receive if the shirt wasn't made in the USA. Fortunately, it was. Great shirt and great pride for a great nation.

To the students who wore US flag clothes to school, I hope nothing breaks your will to be great Americans. Keep up the great work!

Give America A Chance

May 6 Update

1. Whether people don't know their own history or not, I don't know. Why would somebody be offended by somebody else wearing a patriotic shirt in their own country? I don't care what day it is. I wouldn't care if a Mexican tourist was visiting the United States wearing a Mexican flag shirt on the Fourth of July. Why should I? Then again, it wouldn't bother me if somebody was wearing a Union Jack shirt on the Fourth of July.

    I am still shocked by the idea that somebody would get offended by an American symbol in America regardless of the day. Stupid, stupid, stupid!

2. I think the idea is kind of fun in support of our neighboring country. I have nothing against Mexico. I've visited Mexico many times and enjoyed myself every time.

    What I have a problem with is public figures supporting breaking the law. I would fully support, not necessarily agree, but support, the athletes if they were trying to change the law. But promoting the idea of breaking the law, c'mon! Can I say it again…? Stupid!

3. Just to be clear, the shirt wasn't tagged "Made in the USA" (well it was, but hold on…), the "made in" was referring to the baby in the belly that was made in the USA.

May 27, 2010

It's been 3 weeks since I've written. I realize it's my book and I can do what I want, but I feel guilty. To justify myself, I have what I feel is a very good reason… I'm burnt out!

I'm not looking for sympathy, but let me tell you a little bit of what's going on.

The most important thing happening in my life right now is that my wife is pregnant. Fortunately, everything is going very well. My wife is healthy! My daughter is happy! And my household seems to be holding up nicely. However, I constantly wonder if my wife is eating well enough. Is she getting enough rest? Does she have too much stress? You know the normal things men worry about during this time. (1)

We also sold my wife's truck leaving us with one pickup and my Harley. I'm trying to sell the Harley so we can turn the money into a nice family SUV. Hopefully, that'll happen soon. (2)

But the real kicker is work. In addition to my work load increasing significantly, we've implemented a new company policy that adds as LOT of stress. I'm not going to go into details, but I will say that it is a policy that my co-workers are extremely displeased with. When you work with people who are displeased with their job, it kind of rubs off. (3)

Normally, I'm a happy-go-lucky kind of guy, but for some reason, I just can't shake this. (4)

Now I don't want to be a whiner, so I'm doing something about it. Last night, I booked a weeks' vacation in Hawaii. Thank you Priceline.com for getting me tickets at well under half what the airlines were asking. That "bid your own price" deal really paid off! (5)

Give America A Chance

I haven't paid any attention to the news in the past week, so I really don't know what's going on, but as I was walking out to come write tonight, my wife handed me a copy of the Las Cruces Sun News pointing me to a page dealing with the Arizona immigration law. This particular section includes letters written in by locals. There are a few patriots who support the idea of Arizona upholding federal law, but, of course, there's the whiners complaining that it's unfair and we should boycott Arizona. [6]

I came out tonight to solely vent my personal issues hoping that would calm me down. But on the other hand, current news is vital to being a well-rounded American citizen. I just hope you're not the type who believes everything you see and hear. Hopefully, after a de-stressing vacation, I can get back on track. [7]

May 27 Update

1. I'm not as bad as the dads projected in modern television shows, but I do worry a bit about my wife's health... After all, she's carrying my child. Isn't it OK to be a little concerned?
2. I feel it's important to throw something out there... My wife never asked me to sell my Harley... This was my choice alone. In fact, I'm getting the impression that my wife doesn't want me to sell it. I enjoy riding with my wife and without her, it's not the same for me... She can't ride while pregnant and I can't ride with an infant, so it seems silly to keep it at this point.
3. I have to admit that only a few years later, I can't even remember what the policy was. If I really wanted to think about it, I'm sure I could figure it out, but why do that?
4. I really am a happy person... Often times, things upset me, but they don't upset me deeply. I hope that my writing doesn't make it seem like I'm actually running around constantly upset with the world... I truly believe that this is an awesome country to live in. Am I concerned for her future? Yes. Am I concerned about the policies and the "stupidity" of some of the things that happen in this country? Yes. Does it affect me deeply? Heck no... I will do whatever it takes to make my family successful. I won't let others affect my success or my children's success to the best of my ability.
5. I've used Priceline.com many, many times for everything including flights, hotels, and car rentals. The name your own price has really saved me quite a bit of money versus any other site I have ever worked with... You have to be willing to play with it a little bit, though.
6. Boycott an entire state... Yea, that's patriotic. Way to go geniuses.
7. Hawaii... Here I come!

Give America A Chance

June 13, 2010

Today I returned from my much needed vacation. We left on Saturday, June 5th. Our flight arrived early… We had our luggage, rental car, and were on the road well before noon. Let me tell you about it.

My wife and I decided to take the trip because we were both a little burnt out. My daughter was going with her grandparents to Wisconsin at the same time so it worked out perfect. Additionally, tomorrow is our anniversary so it was an early anniversary gift to each other. Timing was right; everything fell into place, so we jumped on the opportunity! [1]

It didn't take us long to decide on visiting the Big Island. We didn't want guided tours, resorts, or expensive dining. After a lot of deliberation, we decided to stay at a bed and breakfast in the "rainforest" side of the island near Hilo, HI. We got a cozy little cottage for the entire week for $500 including tax. Besides the plane tickets, this was the most expensive part of the trip. [1]

After a slow road trip from the airport to our cottage (about 4.5 hours for a hundred mile trip) we called it a day. [2]

We hit up the local farmers markets for our food and only ate at restaurants a few times. Some of the food, like eggs and milk, was quite expensive, but the rest wasn't bad. We got a fresh whole Ahi tuna at a farmers market for 9 bucks and a couple local grass fed rib eye steaks for 12 bucks. Both went great on the grill. [3]

I won't bore you with our day-to-day activities, but one of the other bargains we picked up on was a rental set of snorkel equipment for both of us for the week… 9 bucks. The zoo, factory tours, beaches, waterfall, jungle tours, nighttime lava flows, and lots more were completely free.

I'll get into some of the other things that really "struck" me in the next few days. For now though, I'm exhausted after a long travel day. Good night and God bless!

June 13 Update

1. The entire trip, including airfare, food, lodging, car rental and gas, touring, and souvenirs was under $2,000. Well worth it.
2. The trip was slow simply because we weren't in any sort of a hurry. We stopped at beaches, shops, parks, and pretty much anywhere else we felt like stopping. My wife and I don't generally do too well with guided tours since we're usually the people holding up the rest of the group. So, we didn't book any. We did it our way.
3. I really enjoy buying local. The tuna we bought was from a guy in a boat. I thought that was pretty awesome. I wasn't sure whether or not I'd like tuna since my only exposure to it was the canned stuff that smells and tastes horrible to me… This was no canned tuna. This was amazing.

The cottage we stayed at had a charcoal grill that we made good use of. As an aside, it also had a washer/dryer, full kitchen, and everything else we needed for a very relaxing stay.

June 19, 2010

I've now been back from my vacation for a week. I've completed a normal workweek and although waking up at 5:30am has been tough, the week wasn't too bad. Fortunately, I had really great news on Monday... We're having a boy!!!

My wife's ultrasound was on Monday. I got to see virtually every part of my baby from his head to his fingers and toes. We even got to see his angry face after the tech poked him a little to try and get him to move. Awwww.

Normally, I like to take little notes about things I pick up throughout the week that I want to write about, but I had to purposely avoid that this week since I wanted to talk more about Hawaii.

A good friend of ours went to Hawaii a year before us and was able to give us some great pointers and things to look out for. One of the things he mentioned was picking up mangoes off the ground fresh from the tree. We did that... nothing like the store bought mangoes here in New Mexico.

Another thing he mentioned was trying coconuts. Now, I've tried store-bought coconuts and some foods with coconut in them... neither of which I liked. When we went to the farmers market, he mentioned trying a fresh coconut from one of the locals. I didn't even recognize what a fresh coconut looked like. The gentleman we bought from, Ano was his name, took a coconut and sliced off the top with his machete. OH MY GOODNESS! The "milk" inside was delicious. When we finished that, he cut it in half and made a "spoon" with part of the shell. The insides were more like a fleshy consistency than the dried up crusty coconuts I've tried in the past. The taste was awesome! [1]

Give America A Chance

This leads to the first thing that struck me. Why are we only getting the dried up junk here in New Mexico? Why doesn't Hawaii farm the good stuff and ship it over? As it turns out, most coconut trees have the coconuts cut off and destroyed. Apparently there is a large fear of coconuts falling on people and property. (2)

Another friend wanted us to get her a Hawaiian sarong. We looked all over the farmers markets and stores without luck. At one store, we got excited when we saw some very nice shirts made in Hawaii, but when we asked about the sarong, she said there are none made in Hawaii. She showed us some styles that are designed by Hawaiians, but along with every other sarong, they were made in Indonesia. She said the batik process couldn't be done in the USA, to which my wife responded that she learned how to do it in art class in Wisconsin… that blows the "can't" out of the water, but it gets better. (3)

The sales lady showed us some sarongs that were designed by a Hawaiian couple who live part time in Indonesia where a particular village does the work. Without any prompting, my mind jumped into the possibility of child labor. The sales lady quickly pointed out that no child labor was used and that the Hawaiian designers take very good care of the village they support. They even buy cars and other goods for the villagers and their children. I'm not convinced about the child labor, but that's just my own thoughts. (4)

Many things about the island impressed me like the ability of someone like Ano, for example, who lives completely on the land. The amount of fresh local fruits and vegetables was amazing. I also got to try many of the Kona coffees and local beers, both were great. (5)

But many things were no different than anywhere else in the US. Most of the junk, even at farmers markets, was made in China. We spent a lot of time sorting the genuine Hawaiian made merchandise from the imported junk. (6)

If you go to Hawaii, remember that it's not that different from anywhere else. The same tools, equipment, and toys that you'll find there, you can find anywhere. Try the local foods, but don't waste your time with junk souvenirs. Look for the authentic and you'll be much more satisfied. (7)

June 19 Update

1. And now I'm craving a coconut. I've tried the coconut milk sold in the stores. Not the same.
2. I don't think I fully get this problem... Sure, coconuts falling from the sky would really hurt. On the other hand, Hawaiian coconuts falling from the sky would be worth it. Yep, they were that good.
3. It surprises me that somebody would actually say there's something that Americans can't do.
4. Along the clothing lines, one thing that I wasn't told was that I packed way too many clothes... Apparently, for a week in Hawaii, you can easily get away with a small backpack. A couple shirts (though shirtless works most of the time too), a pair of shorts, swimsuit, and that's about it. Next time, I'm packing light.
Back to the Sarong, though... We ended up buying a few as souvenir gifts. We didn't buy from this store, though... We ended up buying a much cheaper set elsewhere... After all, if they're all made in the same place, why pay more?
5. Ano impressed me in some ways, but not in other ways. In the movie Demolition Man, towards the end, the main character joins the underground city with the above-ground city by telling the above-grounders they needed to get a little dirtier and the under-grounders needed to get a lot cleaner. That statement stuck with me for some reason. I think the bulk of us need to either get a little dirtier in the sense of not being afraid to get our hands dirty and do some real labor or get a little cleaner in the sense of not trying to cook dinner with your own bio-waste (true story).
I'm all about living off the land, but trees grow readily all over the world. That seems like a pretty good option for cooking if you ask me (or any of my ancestors all the way back to Adam and Eve).
6. I noticed this when I went to Africa years ago as well. Chinese merchandise has a stronghold across the globe. That's great for them, but not great for us.
7. This would go for anywhere you like to visit. If you go to France and want a French souvenir, get one, not a Chinese souvenir posing as a French souvenir.

Give America A Chance

June 24, 2010

So I waited almost a week to write again... I didn't think near as much stuff could happen as had happened over the past few days. Between General McChrystal, the disclosure bill, job bill, and basically anything else the Obama team tries to silence and shut up constitutional Americans with.

Freedom of speech. All Americans are entitled to it with a few minor exceptions... when it goes against anything pro-Obama. Well, Mr. Community Organizer, you won't like this! [1]

General McChrystal and his aides may be foul-mouthed, something I don't appreciate, he may be rude, he may be crude, but he is certainly a warrior. This man put his life on the line more times than most to defend this country. To defend my right to say that President Obama screwed up and continues to screw the liberties out of my country. But when General McChrystal told the world that Obama looked nervous in a room full of military brass and Obama's feelings got so hurt, Obama essentially fired him. Silly? No! Dumb? You bet!

Heck, I served in the military (something Obama didn't do), and if you put me in a room full of military people of ANY rank, I get nervous. These are people who have chosen to fight for my safety come life or limb. If you're not nervous, you're either stupid or numb to what our military puts up with. [2]

General McChrystal, thank you for your years of service to my country! [3]

Let's see, what else... Oh, how about adding 33 billion to our nation's deficit. Put another way, how about charging your children's credit card with a $33,000,000,000 fee. Thankfully, the Republicans did what the Democrats proposed... No more money out without money coming in to pay for it. [4]

Oh, sure... the news channels will show people begging on the streets because the "Republicans hate them," but come on people... If you've been on jobless benefits for 2 years, get a job! My local paper is full of page after page of job openings and help wanted ads. McDonald's is hiring. Oh, but wait, you're too proud to work at McDonald's. You'd rather beg on the streets. No, you're a bum! Many people like me are desperately trying to buy American-made products so you have a place to work. Are you? [5]

And how about the disclosure bill that was drafted without disclosure to the American people? Don't forget, Mr. Politician, you work for the American people, not your special interest group. Even the NRA caved into this one. Doesn't surprise me. The NRA constantly fights until they cave in. So what is this bill? [6]

Well, here's one of the simple acts under this bill. It will completely cut special interest contributions to reduce their influence in campaigns... Awesome. The special interest groups got Obama into power. Oh wait, there's more? You're exempt if you have 500,000 members in all 50 states. Whew, Americans can still pull together and use the great groups that started since the Obama charade to pull him out of office. Nope... the bill also says you have to have existed for 10 years already. [7]

So essentially, the Obama train tried to take away more freedom of speech. America, these are your rights that are being ripped from your hands by a man who bows to foreign dictators and shuns elected politicians. You constitution is being ripped to shreds. Your Bills Of Rights are being pulled out from under you. Are you going to sit back and let it happen? I will not! And when push comes to shove, I will shove, kick, punch, and fight for my rights as an American citizen. Don't let a community organizer pull his groups and kick your rights to the curb. Stand up! Become a radical constitutionalist and fight, at all costs, to uphold the rights bestowed to you the day you were conceived in your mother's womb. Do not stand idle while your government tries to push you over and kick you while you're down. Just wait... There's more to this story. [8]

June 24 Update

1. As much as I don't want to make this book about politics, it seems there no way around it. The point of this book is to encourage everybody to buy American-made products. At the same time, there are things happening all around us that seem to try to take the patriotism out of patriots… by force.
2. I honestly don't care if you're a brand-new military member, a career general, or the Commander-in-Chief… If you aren't awestruck by a room full of people willing to die for you, willing to die for your freedoms, something's not right.
3. I mean this honestly. I may not agree with everything you do or how you act every minute of your life, but I do appreciate what you have done for my country.
4. Too bad it was all a lie… Oops, I meant politics.
5. I have no sympathy for those who take advantage of our country's welfare system when they have the ability to get off their lazy butts and GET A JOB!
6. I don't want to criticize the NRA too much. There's a lot to be said for what they have done in this country. Does your city or state honor the second amendment? If so, you should probably thank and support the NRA.
7. I don't know why this stuff surprises me??? I should accept by now that this is just politics as usual, but I don't want to. In fact, I refuse to. I acknowledge that this is politics as usual, but I refuse to accept it. And I will fight to change it.
8. The house passed this bill on June 24, 2010, but failed in the senate on September 23, 2010.

The Rants and Raves of an American Patriot

June 27, 2010

I want to shift gears for a bit. Today we went out with aspirations of getting registered for baby gifts. Many people have been asking what we need/want, so registering seemed like a great idea. We decided to go somewhere where there would be a lot of baby stuff... Babies R Us. (1)

Now before I go into how insulting Chinese R Us was, let me explain some things. I've been on my USA buying rampage for some time now. I'm finding USA items everywhere I go when I'm not looking at plain 'ol junk. I thought finding American-made baby supplies would be a piece of cake... Heck, we've "accidentally" run across American-made car seats and clothes at Sam's Club. Surely Babies R Us could easily compete with that.

Not So! Every single piece of furniture was made in China. Every piece of car accessory was made in China. Clothes? Made in China or Vietnam. Bottles? Heck, even most of them were made in China. It was insulting. When all was said and done, we registered 23 items... pretty much everything in the store that was made in the USA. Now I'm not an over-protective parent. I think kids should get muddy. I think kids should run barefoot and get cuts and scrapes... It's part of growing up. But I don't think kids should be thrown in Chinese junk getting all sorts of who knows what. (2)

There have been 9 million cribs recalled in the past few years including 2 million in the last week. Why? Because we, as parents and consumers, are not demanding quality. I looked at one crib today and found that four small screws were holding the bed onto the so-called wood of the crib. Sure, it looked pretty, but this kind of junk has killed babies. Parents, you have to demand quality. Simply waiting for the recall and their "quick fix" attachment is not going to suffice anymore. Wake up America! (3)

June 27 Update

1. I'll be honest… I chose Babies R Us because I wanted to run around the store and use the laser gun to "tag" everything I wanted. Sounds fun, right?
2. I'm not trying to imply that our kids will get something horrible just by sitting in or wearing merchandise made in China. I am trying to imply that the Chinese wear masks to avoid breathing in unfiltered air from their own country while making products that are going to be packaged and sent to our stores and placed on our kids. It doesn't sound amusing to me. Think of it like this… If you saw a bunch of people running around your area wearing masks filtering the air you're breathing, you'd probably get a little concerned. You'd probably want to either put on a mask or leave the area. Would you take a blanket you found in the same area and place it on your kids?
3. Parents can't do this alone… They need the teamwork of all parents and non-parents alike. They need the teamwork of Americans. In case you're still wondering, that's you!

June 29, 2010

Let me ask you a quick question… What holiday will we as Americans be celebrating at the beginning of next month (July)? Did you answer "The 4th of July" or "Independence Day"? Another question… why do we celebrate it? I'll let you dwell on that awhile. Unfortunately, I'm extremely short on time tonight. I've got some great things to talk about though. Hopefully tomorrow. Good night and God bless!

June 30, 2010

Have you gone out and seen Toy Story 3 yet? That was really a great movie. My family and I went to see it earlier this evening and really enjoyed it. It was clean. It was family oriented. There was no swearing (which is really awesome for a movie in this era). And there were good messages. If you haven't seen it, go check it out. It's worth it. [1]

As I get closer to the end of my one-year point for writing this book, I start thinking of the things I should (or shouldn't have) written. Well, I'm not going to go back and change anything. I said what was on my mind at that particular time and I'll stick to my guns. If I'm proven wrong at some point, I will gladly accept responsibility and acknowledge that I was incorrect. For the most part, I firmly believe what I've written and the overall message of this book… Buy American products! Protect the things that make this country great. And honor those who fight the good fight. But most of all, be good to yourself and your neighbor.

Yesterday, I met one of my neighbors. She was a very nice woman with whom I could see becoming friends with… and her entire family once I meet them. She showed me pictures of her two sons, both of which are Eagle Scouts. Being an Eagle Scout myself, I know the amount of work and time required to make it. We talked about quite a few things from gardening to owning your own business… which brings up an exciting topic.

The family seems to be a very active family. They drive classic cars, are master skiers, and play a lot in the water with kayaks and sailboats.

The woman got sick and tired of buying Chinese junk and "one size fits all" parts for their "toys." But rather than sit and complain like a whiner, she decided to open up shop… literally.

She is starting a business so that she can make all the custom parts necessary to keep her family's hobbies running smoothly. She's also planning on advertising these custom-made parts for others to enjoy. Talk about the American dream! Once she gets up and running, I'll provide her some free advertising right here in my book. [2]

One thing completely off topic that I've forgotten to mention is that we got ourselves a new truck. Not brand new, but new to us. A friend of mine sold us their 2005 Chevrolet Suburban. So far it's been a great truck and it was built in Wisconsin… how great is that! Even better, I got to keep my money right here in the community. We're ready for some road trips now… Here we come America! [3]

Also, I'm not going to answer my June 29 questions right now, but I will add to them. Do you know what significant event happened in summer, 1776? I hope most Americans are answering an astounding 'YES!' But I don't know what exactly they're teaching in schools nowadays. Let me get a bit tougher… When did we, as the United States of America become a country? When did George Washington become the president of the United States of America? And lastly, what system of government do we, as Americans, operate under? I hope you know the answers to these, but if you don't, you may be in for a surprise.

June 30 Update

1. It seems like more and more, my wife and I are switching to older movies rather than opting for the newer movies that are being released lately. The reason is simple… they made good movies years ago. At least "better" movies, in my opinion. There wasn't the need to add foul language or "innuendo." Why is it that so many movies lately, even kid's movies, add this sort of material? I have a suspicion, but it's probably better kept to myself.
2. Jerilyn Remley created Enchanted Woodworks. Look for her business online. Support a fellow American.
3. And come we did… We took a major road trip, filled the 8 passenger suburban to near capacity and had an awesome 3,000 mile road trip with my family as well as my niece and nephews. We still have the suburban and it's still running strong.

The Rants and Raves of an American Patriot

July 2, 2010

Sometimes the ignorant surprise me about how ignorant they can be…

Today was Friday. The last day of work before a long holiday weekend. So while I was at work, I monitored some of the topics being discussed on Fox News. What I heard simply astounded me. Put simply, I heard a discussion taking place between two gentlemen. One was a democrat. The other was a republican. The discussion was about the massive unemployment we have in our country right now. The democrat was saying that we, as Americans, can create jobs quickly by paying people more not to work and the "republicans want the economy to fail." The republican tried arguing that paying people not to work would keep unemployment steady or worse and "republicans want the US economy to succeed." [1]

So what is this all about? Apparently, Nancy Pelosi stated that "unemployment checks are a fast way to create jobs." So who's right? I'm going to try to keep my "spin" off the subject and let you decide. I've can see pro's and con's to both sides.

If you pass out more unemployment checks to the jobless, there is more money in circulation. More money being passed around communities creates jobs. Stores have to hire workers to sell the products and people have to make the products. It may also mean that people can fix up their houses and others may have the money to buy one.

There are problems to this though. Unemployment checks are normally not that much. On average, people can make more money working and actually earning their income. When people take a reduction in pay, they usually buy more "throw-away" cheap temporary stuff… Chinese junk. So you're not creating more American jobs. [2]

Additionally, there may be pressure for some to give up their jobs in lieu of unemployment checks. If you were offered a 30% cut in pay not to work, would you take it? If it was offered to my wife, I would beg her to take it and be an at-home mom—even if it was only temporary.

Republicans are generally about smaller government and larger personal responsibility. I would guess that the Republican solution would be to provide unemployment checks on an extremely temporary basis… say 6 months for example. Lower each check monthly so the unemployed get more and more desperate for jobs until they're forced to work anywhere. McDonald's, for example, they're always hiring. That would lessen the economic burden of the unemployed on the U.S. government, but it doesn't help in the long run. [3]

To help in the long run, you would need to significantly lower taxes on the business owners so they could afford to hire more employees. And if there was less bureaucracy in creating a business, more people would be inclined to open their own businesses. [4]

That solution isn't perfect either. Perhaps if politicians cared less about their party lines and more about the welfare of the citizens they represent, they could find a happy medium. Unfortunately, I think both sides are being too dang stubborn! [5]

The simple fact is, you can't pay people not to work and expect them to support our economy and you can't give business owners more breaks and expect them to hire more employees.

The solution… we, as Americans, need to figure that out. I'll think about my ideas and pass them on, but you need to do the same. After all, politicians aren't geniuses.

July 2 Update

1. It bugs me when people try to throw another person or party under the bus with general terms. "Republicans are trying to ruin the country." "Democrats are trying to ruin the country." Where's the value in those statements? Do people actually fall for this?
2. Not so good anymore, right? If you're looking for a short-term solution that will end up worse in the long run, this sounds great. It's kind of like sweeping the dirt under the rug so the floor looks clean. Everything looks great now, but after time, that dirt is going to eat away at the flooring and you'll have to replace the entire flooring.
3. I hate to say desperate, but I think that's how it needs to be discussed sometimes. If anybody's been taking unemployment checks for more than 6 months, there's something wrong. It's nice to have some backup when you get laid off, but c'mon… 6- months???
4. Have you ever worked for a poor person?
5. When will our politicians figure this out? I don't care what letters follow your name. I don't care about the generalities that you throw out. I don't care that your resume says that you put the needs of the people in front of your party lines… I want to see the proof… And honestly, I don't see much proof… Do you remember when John McCain kept telling us that, as president, he would carry his red marker and highlight all of the pork spending on every bill he received? How about doing that now? And while you're at it, stop putting your own pork in the bills.

Give America A Chance

July 3, 2010

Tomorrow is the 234th anniversary of what could quite possibly be the most important day in American history! On July 4th, 1776, the thirteen states (colonies) that made up the United States of America at the time, unanimously declared independence from Great Britain. The men who signed the Declaration of Independence sealed their fate with a pledge on their lives, fortune, and sacred honor. [1]

Today, we don't think much about that day. We shoot off fireworks, drink too much, and have a great big bar-b-que with our friends and neighbors. All too often, we forget about the men who died for our freedom. The men who signed the Declaration of Independence knew exactly what they were doing and believe me; they were shaking in their boots to do such a brave thing. Many of those men were hunted down, tortured, and murdered. Their families may have been tortured and murdered as well, just to set an example. [2]

I hope that tomorrow, in your celebrations, you remember the men and women who fought to maintain our freedom and independence from any sort of rule over our free nation. Read the Declaration of Independence. Seriously, right now, go read the Declaration of Independence.

I went out with my family today and bought fireworks. I'm fully aware that most "small time" fireworks are made in China, but like many Americans, I like the ability to celebrate by shooting off fireworks, having a grand bar-b-que, and spending the day with family and friends. Tomorrow is also a Sunday, so I'm eager to see what my church has in store for a sermon. [3]

Allow me some time to describe a person whom I will most certainly never meet in person.

This person refused to agree to laws that would promote public good.

This man did not allow his governors to pass laws of immediate importance.

This man created judges that operate for his standards alone.

This man created new offices and positions that limit the freedoms of America.

This man called together private meetings to create laws that forced Americans into compliance.

Do you know who I am talking about? This man was the king of Great Britain. He was the ruler of the country that, until July 4, 1776, tyrannically controlled our great nation. The description I gave came from the submitted facts in the Declaration of Independence. [4]

If you know of any person in our modern day political atmosphere that comes close to that description, you need to be frightened. Our government was instituted by Americans and gets their power only from the consent of us, as Americans. According to the Declaration of Independence, it is "the right of the people to alter or abolish" any form of government that does not protect our life, liberty, and our pursuit of happiness. Just remember, the keyword there is the pursuit of happiness. Our government was not set up to guarantee our happiness. [5]

Please, I beg of you, remember what made and continues to make this country great. Teach your children the importance of freedom and our nation's history.

So now you know what I pray you already knew. There was once a tyrant who tried to take away your freedom. But our forefathers, heroes of this country, pledged that they would take tyranny no more. They gave EVERYTHING so that nothing could be taken from you. Would you do the same?

Give America A Chance

July 3 Update

1. They put their lives on the line for what they believed... All I'm asking is that you choose to change who you give your money to.
2. I don't know exactly what happened to the people and the families of those men who signed the Declaration of Independence, but, without a doubt, it wasn't something that they did expecting wonderful and lucrative gifts from the king of Great Britain. I've heard that some were tortured for their signing and I've hear that the "torture" was simply harsh conditions given to all prisoners given during wartime. In either case, their actions proved that they were willing to die for what they believed in.
3. I'm not different than most other Americans... I want my kids to see fancy lights bursting in the sky. I want my kids to spend time with friends celebrating the fact that they can spend time with their friends and shoot fire in the sky. Am I willing to spend a few bucks on Chinese-made products for that, sure... I'm not too happy about that part though.
4. When I first read through this list, I thought of somebody else altogether. Mainly, every single politician I have ever met.
5. Our freedoms are guaranteed by the constitution of the United States of America, not given by them. Guaranteed... meaning, nobody, including our government can take them away. And when they do, they are in the wrong.

July 5, 2010

Well, I didn't get to write yesterday, but I had an awesome Independence Day celebration. [1]

We started the day at church and let me tell you, hearing a congregation of God fearing Americans singing "God Bless America" is enough to get you choked up and fired up at the same time.

Then we had a fantastic sermon about "Americas past—A Roadmap for our future." I'll get to that.

Then, our church celebrates communion on the first Sunday of every month. The opportunity to recognize my personal savior's promise to me on my country's celebrated day of independence was truly awe-inspiring and totally awesome! [2]

First, let me answer the questions from June 30th. When did we, as the United States of America, become a country? There's some light-hearted discussion about this. Some don't recognize July 4, 1776 as that ever-important date. On June 21, 1788, New Hampshire became the 9th state to ratify our constitution. According to Article 7 of the U.S. Constitution, nine states were required to establish the U.S. Constitution. Could that be our birthday? Here's my simple answer, right or wrong, I say July 4, 1776 is our country's birthday. This is the day we declared ourselves an independent nation.

When did George Washington become president of the United States of America? April 30, 1789. However, we operated as a confederated nation for 15 years before George Washington. And, there were 14 presidents, loosely defined, before George Washington. Now don't go around telling people that Ol' George wasn't our first president. Under the U.S. Constitution, he most certainly was our first elected president. Confused yet?

Give America A Chance

How could we have presidents between our first president and the birth of our nation? It's simple really.

We became our own country when we declared it to be so. [3]

But we went through a growing period. Before the U.S. Constitution, still in effect today, we were under the Articles of Confederation. The "presidents" under the Articles of Confederation provided a weak system of government during our growing period. Not until the U.S. Constitution did we find our governing doctrine of today and the first president under that government. [4]

What system of government do we, as Americans, operate under? We operate as a republic… Remember the Pledge of Allegiance? "And to the Republic for which it stands." Surprise!!! We're not a democracy. If you don't know what a republic is, you'll have to look it up. Government 101 is more than I plan on going into in a couple short paragraphs. Very loosely, however, it means we elect people to speak on our behalf. Just wait until you learn about the Electoral College… that's a whole other ball of wax.

I'll have to go into the fantastic church sermon at another time. It's late and I want to go to bed. Remember this, though. It's now 234 years and 1 day since our country became an independent, free nation. Let's keep it that way!

July 5 Update

1. There's something great about saying that… Our country is independent. We have our independence. Independence from what? Well, to me, it's a whole lot more than just independence from a king long since dead.
2. Many men have died to provide this country freedom. Only one died to set your soul free!
3. We didn't become a free country because we asked for it… We became a free country because we demanded it. We fought for it. So yes, we get to choose the day we became an independent country.
4. As an aside, our country tried out many different types of "presidents" from far left-wing to far right-wing. We chose a system of government somewhere in the middle. Today, that middle ground would be extremely left-wing. Perhaps that's why so many call the constitution an outdated piece of paper. Personally, I like that piece of paper and think we should honor it. If you want to know where I stand politically, I stand behind our constitution.

July 13, 2010

The past week has been another one of my busy weeks. We're trying to get our apartment ready so a friend can move in, but working on a budget means I do most of the work. I'm also trying to build a chicken coop so we can have a good supply of fresh eggs. It's all quite enjoyable work actually.

So before I run out of time, let me talk about my Independence Day church sermon.

The main focus of the sermon was "If we forget who we were, we will forget who we are." The many quotes of which I cannot all reprint here, testify to the fact that America was founded by God-fearing people. [1]

George Washington said that "It is impossible to govern rightly without God and the Bible." Many people like to throw around the phrase "separation of Church and State." Do you know where that phrase comes from? It's not the Constitution and it's not the Declaration of Independence. [2]

In a letter that Thomas Jefferson wrote to the Danbury Baptist Association, he states:

> I contemplate with sovereign reverence that act of the whole American people which declared that their legislature should make no law respecting an establishment of religion, or prohibiting the free exercise thereof, thus building a wall of separation between Church and State.

The letter continues and I encourage you to look it up and read it in its entirety for yourselves. Basically, the "separation of Church and State" does not mean that the state must be separate from the church. In fact, it's nearly the opposite. It guarantees our right to be part of any church we wish to be a part of… State included. It does mean, however, that the state cannot force us into any type of church. [3]

My pastor also mentioned there seems to be a focus in our media that "rather than pride, we're supposed to feel guilty" as Americans. He pointed out that God has used America to keep other nations free. God has used America to provide relief for the suffering. Simply look at how much Americans have poured out with their time, money, and labor to help out Haiti after their terrible earthquake.

Unfortunately, the public school system, media, and many others have tried to change history to take out much of our religious freedoms. Alexis de Toequeville came to America in the 1800's to find out what makes America great. His conclusion, "America is great because America is good, and if America ever ceases to be good, America will cease to be great."

So what made America good? "Upon my arrival in the United States, the religious aspect of the country was the first thing that struck my attention; and the longer I stayed there, the more did I perceive the great political consequences resulting from this state of things." [4]

Well, I've been preaching some of what was preached to me long enough. I do whole-heartedly believe that America is good. We're not good because of who we are alone though, we're good because we've built our nation on the basis of the Ten Commandments. We're good because we are a nation built by good people. Try as they may, nobody can erase our history; only distort it to the ignorant and uneducated people who refuse to think on their own. [5]

Give America A Chance

July 13 Update

1. I want to throw an aside before I start re-telling you the sermon. Much of what was said is something that I not only believe in, but something that I've researched in the past and knew was true. I wouldn't repeat it if I didn't believe it to be true.

2. It surprises me how many people believe that the separation of church and state is part of the governing law of our nation. And when they do believe it, they want to rely on our Constitution. Everything else, they want to throw under the bus.

3. Simply stated, Jefferson was saying that the United States will not force a religion on its people, but at the same time, nobody can force the religion out of its people.

4. When people came to this country, they noticed a religious guidance for the people. They noticed that the people tried to be good people. We're they perfect? Nope. Will we ever be perfect? Not a chance.

    I want to throw out something a little different for a second. For the most part, I've been trying to keep my updated commentary relevant to the particular paragraph at hand, but something happened over this past weekend that I really don't want to ignore (and it kind of fits since I mentioned schools).

    Yesterday, a local public school teacher died suddenly of a heart attack. It was a tragedy to say the least. With school starting back up on Monday, it's going to be difficult for the teaching staff that worked with him as well as all the students. To help, many of the local pastors were asked to come in tomorrow and counsel those who need it. I think it's an awesome thing to provide.

    What is really interesting to me is that while we, as a "modern" culture, push harder and harder to remove God from our government and our schools, we recognize the need for God when a crisis happens. There's comfort in the truth of God. I don't want to harp on this, but it's something I think warrants a lot more attention.

5. A friend of mine told me a story about a conversation he had with another man. Apparently, the other man was complaining about Christian day care centers, arguing that he would never send his child to one of "those" places. My friend asked the disgruntled gentleman which of the Ten Commandments he disagrees with. "Is it the "thou shalt not kill" that you disagree with? How about the adultery? Or the stealing?"

July 16, 2010

I've been feeling a little guilty because I haven't talked about American-made items in a while. Honestly, I really haven't bought much of anything worth mentioning. We've obviously bought food and necessities, but nearly everything else has been second hand stuff from re-sale stores and garage sales. I'm hesitant to talk about that sort of stuff in detail because time changes things. The hand tools that I bought at a garage sale that say made in USA on them may have been from 50 years ago. The president of the company that makes them has probably been replaced by a board of directors who care more about the bottom line than the American citizen.

I did, however, buy a nice 25' Stanley measuring tape made in the USA. It was new, but even Stanley sold out on some of their other products.

So do I have a point to this? Sure… If you shop at re-sale stores and garage sales, you can often get quality made, USA made, merchandise that will probably last you longer than the new Chinese equivalent. You're still putting Americans to work, you're still supporting your community, but you're not supporting the greedy sell-out businessmen who moved their production lines to communist nations.

I'll give you an example… Last week, my wife went to Goodwill. She came across a baby crib that was in nearly new condition, American-made, and extremely well designed. On top of that, she got a brand new, still in the wrapper, made in USA crib mattress for $30. In my eyes it doesn't get much better than that. [1]

And now, I've got something more personal to share… and ask. Last week, I had a dream that woke me up angry and confused. I'll tell the short story about it.

Give America A Chance

My wife and I were driving down the California coast on the way to a doctor's appointment. We saw a dozen men get out of a boat and into a large van. I was able to count out a dozen men who I knew had just been smuggled illegally into my country.

I was angry by the act and became more furious with the thought that there was nobody I could call to report this crime. California wouldn't enforce the law, heck; Arizona is essentially being sued by President Obama for enforcing the law.

The men drove out of sight speeding off ahead of us. But we saw them again at the doctor's office. I was more than furious. I was downright angry. These illegal aliens broke into my country and were now using my tax dollars to get medical care, not to mention making us wait. After waiting two hours, providing insurance, and paying our co-pay, we left the clinic.

When we got back in our vehicle, I spotted a couple people hiding in the back of our Suburban. We pulled over and I violently pulled them from the back into my view. I was surprised to see it was a young girl, probably about 10 years old. She and her much younger brother were begging for mercy. I told her no… Her and her brother were illegal aliens and needed to be sent to law enforcement. She pleaded with me telling me that their parents were murdered by the Mexican gangs and that they wanted to kill them too.

I sat astonished, contemplating what to do. As children, I figured that law enforcement would probably send them back into Mexico into some sort of orphanage or something… a death sentence for the children.

And now I wake up… angry and confused. How different would that same scenario be in real life? Would California authorities actually act on a 911 call for suspected illegal aliens? Would a Mexican gang actually pursue children? Honestly, I don't know. And that's where I start wondering about our humanity as Americans. I don't question whether or not Americans are good people… we are! But our laws, especially those enforced, are good for humanity. Does our court system genuinely have the ability to determine right from wrong when innocence is at stake? Not just when someone can afford a high-priced lawyer. [2]

July 16 Update

1. That crib has now lasted for two baby boys and the mattress is still being used in a Little Tykes toddler "race car" bed, made in the USA.
2. I don't want to add comment to this. It was a dream that made me wonder for some time and I hope I'm never put into a situation like this because it would tear me apart to figure out what to do. On one hand, I can't just "adopt" a couple orphans without breaking the law myself. On the other hand, it would be nearly impossible to turn innocent children over to what could be catastrophic to their lives.

Give America A Chance

July 27, 2010

As I get closer to the end of my one-year discussion, I realized a few things. First, I've purchased far fewer things than when I started. Quite simply, that's because I've been a homeowner for about 13 months now and I've either purchased most things that I needed or I've given up (like the wall sconce for example). [1]

Secondly, I've focused a whole lot more politically than I intended. That was probably inevitable with our president and congress pretty much screwing everything up. [2]

Thirdly, I've focused more religiously than I intended. I mentioned this earlier, but there also seems to be some sort of war against the one true God in this world… and that's a war that I will proudly be on the front line for.

When I've purchased things, I tried to be candid in my remarks about them. Recently, I've purchased very few things except necessities and things I've already written about. My most recent purchase that's worth writing about was baseboards. I purchased new baseboards made by LP Building Products that were, of course, made in the USA.

Politically, it seems nothing has changed lately. President Obama keeps lying and throwing our country deeper and deeper down the toilet. I don't know if he's just ignorant to all the errors and lies or if he doesn't care. More likely than either of those two, he's probably pretty much worthless. He doesn't have the ability to fix what's wrong but if he can just spend more money, he feels like he's doing something… anything. [3]

Religiously, there's a war rising. Christian values, you know, those pesky Ten Commandments, are being fought right and left. Rather than raising a culture with values and morals, people are raising their kids to accept the perverse. Little girls are getting pregnant and their schools are helping to hide it from their families. I know of one parent whose child was marked "present" for class, driven 3 hours to get a taxpayer funded abortion. No parent approval or prior knowledge. Yet they send home an approval slip for a field trip to a science lab in some cities.

People aren't taking responsibility for their actions. Heck, people aren't even taking responsibility for their own attitude. "I was raised by a single parent" or "that's just the fiery red-head in me." Charles Swindoll said "the remarkable thing is we have a choice every day regarding the attitude we will embrace for that day." Amen to that! [4]

Mr. Swindoll also says that "life is 10% what happens to me and 90% how I react to it." Have you ever heard the saying that you should write down 5 goals and stick it to your mirror? Every morning, if you read and believe in your goals, you will be much more likely to achieve them. So if you believe over and over that since you were raised by a single parent, you won't be successful, you're probably right.

A religious lecture isn't necessary to know that we need to straighten up our own lives first before helping others achieve success in their own lives. I hear people over and over say that they don't go to church because it's full of hypocrites. You know what, they're right. I go to church. I believe in the Ten Commandments. Am I perfect, no! Church goers may be hypocrites, but they try to be better people than the people they once were.

Give it a shot, you may find that if you go with an open mind and an open heart, you'll find people just like you… trying to be better individuals and citizens. That's part of my goal in life… What's yours?

July 27 Update

1. Years later, I still don't have an American-made wall sconce. I'm sure they're out there, but I couldn't find one.
2. This book wasn't meant to be political, but it happened. It seems impossible to think back now and imagine writing a book about America without being political, but I intended to give it a shot… can you say major failure?
3. If you can't tell, it really bugs me when the leaders of our country put their politics in front of their citizens. I don't foresee any sort of "kumbaya" meeting between the Republicans and Democrats, but I would really like to see them quit blaming each other for their own mistakes.
4. I don't care what your religious values are; you can obviously find something wrong with that scenario. I won't get on my soap box about the lies the abortion clinics tell about their safety or about how they ignore the physiological needs of the women they hurt. I don't want to use this book to explain the need to openly invite God back into America.

    I want to use this book to tell you that if you want this country to succeed, if you want your country to prosper, you need to support Americans. If you're a politician, you need to put your politics behind you and do what's best for your citizens, even if it means voting outside your party lines. If you're an "average Joe," like me, it means you need to buy American products, help your neighbor, and encourage your friends to do the same. It's not that you should do it… it's that you NEED to do it.

    We're failing. We're hurting. We're falling apart. It's up to us to fix us.
5. Having responsibility for your own attitude is something I teach my kids. It shouldn't have to be something I tell full grown adults. Your attitude is the one thing that NOBODY can take away from you. Many will try to take it from you. Some will try very, very hard. Don't let them take what belongs to you.

Today

This is not my last chapter. I will continue to support Americans by supporting American businesses. This book is a call to action. I am an American patriot and I am calling YOU.

How will you respond?

www.ingramcontent.com/pod-product-compliance
Lightning Source LLC
LaVergne TN
LVHW061251060426
835507LV00017B/2008